PAULINES AND PASTORALS

THE ERASTUS PAVEMENT

PAULINES
AND
PASTORALS

BY

P. N. HARRISON, D.D., D.LITT.

WIPF & STOCK · Eugene, Oregon

Wipf and Stock Publishers
199 W 8th Ave, Suite 3
Eugene, OR 97401

Paulines and Pastorals

By Harrison, P. N.
ISBN 13: 978-1-5326-0021-0
Publication date 6/3/2016
Previously published by Villiers Publications, 1964

PREFACE

For quite a long time I had been preparing a second edition of The Problem of the Pastoral Epistles, which was to have shown how far I am still convinced, after so many years, that the solution I proposed in 1921 is sound, and how far I now see reason to adopt at certain points a modified form of that solution.

Many pages of the first edition are still the best I can do, and were to have been reproduced without any change. Many others need only a few minor corrections. In some pages a whole paragraph had to be re-written or replaced by a new one. But others no longer express my considered opinion, and could well be omitted, leaving room for much new material now to hand.

At last all was ready for the Press. But I then learned that the cost of printing such a work today, with its very large Appendices, consisting of lists of Greek words and technical symbols, would necessitate a selling price for each copy of at least four times the 12/6 for which the first edition was still available. This would obviously have been prohibitive for many of those who, I had hoped, would someday be numbered among its readers.

For this reason it seemed best to give up the idea of a second edition, at any rate for the present, till stocks of the 1921 edition were exhausted, and instead to bring out a new book consisting of the fresh material, as a sequel to the other.

The present volume, then, is intended to serve a dual purpose. (1) Assuming that its readers are acquainted with my previous work on the Pastoral Epistles, and can refer to it if they wish, they may now learn which of those earlier pages express what their author still holds as firmly as when they were written, which of them I myself regard as obsolete, and at which points I now wish to make corrections and amendments. (2) The rest of this volume is devoted to linguistic data of which I was unaware in 1921, and modifications of my original hypothesis designed to account for them.

My sincere thanks are due to Mr. Martin Harrison for permission to use his photograph of the Erastus pavement at Corinth, taken in 1954.

Bournemouth,
  July, 1963

CONTENTS

APPENDICES

CHAPTER I

INTRODUCTORY

This companion volume and supplement to 'The Problem of the Pastoral Epistles' is the result of more time and effort, devoted since 1921 to further research, than went to the making of that first essay. In the course of these studies many facts hitherto unknown to me have emerged, throwing new light on the solution I proposed forty three years ago.

1. To a certain extent the nature of this fresh evidence, and its bearing upon our problem, has already been indicated in articles of mine (1) reviewing Spicq, *Les Épitres Pastorales* (Journal of Theological Studies, XLIX, 1948), (2) *Onesimus and Philemon* (Anglican Theological Review, October 1950), (3) *The Authorship of the Pastoral Epistles* (The Expository Times, December 1955), and (4) *The Pastoral Epistles and Duncan's Ephesian Theory* (New Testament Studies, Vol. 2, No. 4, Cambridge, May 1956).

Spicq's massive volume is probably the most learned and thorough presentation of the traditional view. So in pointing out where his arguments fail to meet the case, one was at the same time showing why 'Critical' scholars remain unconvinced when other 'Conservatives' use the same arguments.

'Onesimus and Philemon' included a first attempt to show how the problem of Colossians may be solved by a greatly simplified form of H. J. Holtzmann's famous theory, that in this Epistle a genuine letter to the church at Colossae was interpolated by the author of Ephesians, who himself borrowed even more from that original letter than from all the other Paulines.

The Expository Times article was one of a series under the title 'Important Hypotheses Reconsidered'. In it the case for dating the Pastorals towards the end of Trajan's life, and in the earlier years of Hadrian's reign, is shown to be stronger than ever, now that lists can be given both of words and of phrases in these Epistles, all of which were demonstrably in use during that period, whereas no evidence is forthcoming that any of them were current in Paul's lifetime or earlier. Linguistically the Pastorals have more in common with writings of the eighty eight years A.D. 90–178 than with the vastly larger body of Greek literature from Homer downwards till A.D. 90. At the same time I was able to give a much simpler and better account than in 1921 of the Genuine Notes embodied in 2 Timothy. Instead of four such notes assigned to as many different occasions, I now find only two, consisting of the same verses as before, but somewhat differently distributed. This became possible when, thanks to Dr. G. S. Duncan ('St. Paul's Ephesian Ministry', London, 1929), I came to see that Paul's letters to Philemon and to the church at Colossae were written not in Rome but at Ephesus.

On the other hand I have never been able to follow Duncan in his contention that Philippians, Ephesians and the genuine matter embodied in 2 Timothy were also written during that same period. My reasons for this were given in New Testament Studies, May 1956. See below, Chapter X.

2. Now, as in 1921, the main argument turns on a comparison of the language of the Pastorals with that of the genuine letters of St. Paul. But whereas I then believed that our ten Paulines were all of them written or dictated by the Apostle himself, the fresh evidence now available has convinced me (1) that Ephesians was written not by Paul but by Onesimus of Colossae, who c. A.D. 90 took a leading part at Ephesus in collecting Paul's letters, as maintained by John Knox and E. J. Goodspeed – see below, Chapter VI – (2) that at the same time and place Onesimus added certain interpolations to the original letter which Paul had written, also at Ephesus, to the church at Colossae, and sent along with Philemon by the hand of Tychicus – see below, Chapter VII – (3) that Romans i. 19-ii. 1 is an interpolation of about the same date as the Pastorals – see below, Chapter VIII – (4) I share the doubts of many other scholars about the authenticity of 2 Thessalonians.

3. One direct result of these conclusions – especially of (1) above – and of the linguistic data on which they are based, is

10

that we can now recognize in Onesimus our earliest and most important 'external witness' to the authenticity of eight Pauline Epistles, including the three pages or so of Paul's original letter to the church at Colossae, and the twenty five pages of Romans remaining after the single page specified above (3) has been omitted, but not 2 Thessalonians. Another result is to heighten still further the contrast between the language of these genuine Paulines and that of the Pastorals as shown in Part II of P.P.E.

4. It is here maintained that Romans xvi was sent by St. Paul not to Rome but to Ephesus, consisting as it does, first, of a brief note introducing its bearer Phoebe to members of that church, then of greetings from the Apostle and his companions at Corinth (including Erastus) to special friends at Ephesus, with a warning against mischief-makers there. This fits in well with the idea that Phoebe carried with her at the same time a second copy (made by Tertius for the church at Ephesus) of Rom. i-xv, to which Rom. xvi is thus a sort of postscript and covering note combined. See below, Chapter IX.

5. A case is now submitted for regarding as one and the same person (a) the Erastus whom Paul sent with Timothy from Ephesus into Macedonia (Acts xix. 22), (b) the Erastus who, as steward or clerk of the works, (not 'treasurer') at Corinth, sent greetings to his old friends at Ephesus (Rom. xvi. 23), (c) the Erastus who stayed on at Corinth when Paul left that city (2 Tim. iv. 20), and (d) the Erastus who twenty five years or so later, as deputy, in the temporary absence of his chief the aedile or superintendent of public works at Corinth, laid at his own expense the pavement discovered in 1929 by American excavators. See below, Chapter XI.

6. Had it been possible to issue now a second edition of 'The Problem of the Pastoral Epistles', (a) the following eighty pages of the first edition would have been reproduced without change – ii, vi, vii, 1, 3-5, 14-18, 24-26, 28, 31-33, 41, 47, 54-56, 59-64, 67, 69, 72, 75 f., 90-92, 94, 97, 101 f., 105-110, 113, 116, 130, 141 f., 145 f., 150-6, 159, 166-79, 181 f., 184, (also Appendix IV, fourteen pages of Text).

(b) On forty seven pages the only changes were very small

11

ones, with which I need not trouble the reader. Many of these were made necessary by my regrettable failure to notice a misprint in Moulton and Geden's Concordance to the Greek Testament, pointed out in their Corrigenda (as explained in my article in The Expository Times). The word ὑβρίζω occurs of course not in 1 Timothy but in 1 Thess. ii. 2. The corrections required by this error, though surprisingly numerous, are much too minute to have any effect at all on the argument. For the same reason I pass over many small verbal improvements. The pages in question are i, iii-v, 9 f., 19-23, 27, 29 f., 34, 36 f., 40, 43-6, 50 f., 57 f., 68, 70 f., 73 f., 87-89, 93, 95 f., 98 f., 112, 114, 117, 129, 132, 144, 157, 185 (=Appendix IV, i).

(c) Larger changes, running sometimes to a paragraph or more, were necessary on fifty six pages – viii-x, 2, 6-8, 11-13, 35, 38 f., 42, 48 f., 52 f., 65 f., 77 f., 80, 82, 100, 103 f., 111, 115, 118 f., 126-8, 131, 133 f., 135-40, 143, 147-9, 158, 160-5, 180, 183. For the more important among those on pp. 1-81 see Chapter II.

(d) Twelve pages were marked for deletion – 79, 81, 83-6, 120-5 – making room for Appendix II E and F, and in part for Excursuses I-IV. These Excursuses are now replaced by new Chapters VI-XI.

CHAPTER II

PARAGRAPHS NEW OR RE-WRITTEN
(Replacing those in P.P.E. pp. 1-81)

(1) P.P.E. p. 6¹³. It is now agreed by the overwhelming majority of conservative scholars that these epistles cannot by any means be fitted into the known life of St. Paul as recorded in Acts[1].

★   ★   ★

(2) P.P.E. p. 7³⁻⁷. (a) Phrases borrowed from the ten Paulines ... and (b) the 'Personalia' in 2 Timothy and Titus. ... In these two respects, and to this extent, the language of the Pastorals is indeed Paul's own. But for the rest they are written in the Hellenistic Greek of the first half of the second century, and include a number of words and phrases certainly current then, but not, so far as we know, in Paul's day.

★   ★   ★

(3) P.P.E. p. 8¹⁰⁻²⁹ the real author of the Pastorals was a devout, sincere and earnest Paulinist, who wrote at Ephesus during the later years of Trajan and the earlier years of Hadrian's reign. He knew and had studied deeply every one of our ten Paulines. In addition to these he had access to three personal communications sent by the Apostle to his helpers Timothy and Titus, preserved by them till their death, and then bequeathed as a priceless heirloom either to the Church or to some trusted friend at Ephesus.

Two of them were brief notes written not long after Paul left Ephesus for the last time. The third was his Last Letter and Farewell to Timothy, written in Rome not long after

---

[1]That this can be done, while maintaining their Pauline authorship, was once held by a very few scholars, notably Vernon Bartlet in '*The Historic Setting of the Pastoral Epistles*' (Expositor, 8th Series, Vol. V, pp. 47, 161, 256, 325, London, 1913 – superseding what he wrote in his 'Apostolic Age') – but not, so far as I know, by any living writer.

Philippians, on the eve, or possibly on the very day, of his martyrdom. Our 2 Timothy, which was the first of the three Pastorals to be written, consists of this Last Letter expanded by the *auctor ad Timotheum* to meet the requirements of his own day, with a shorter note, which had really been written some six years earlier, inserted between its fourth and fifth paragraphs. Our Titus also has a genuine Note appended in iii, 12-15.

*   *   *

(4) P.P.E. p. 8^{39} – 9^1. Our author was acquainted with the Synoptic tradition and probably with Acts, Philo. (See below, Appendix II E), 1 Peter (P.P.E. p. 175), and 1 Clement (P.P.E. p. 177).

*   *   *

(5) p. 12^{41} there is, indeed, no reason to suppose that he did deceive anybody.

*   *   *

(6) p. 12^{26}-13^6. The Pastorals, then, are neither 'genuine' (meaning the first-hand work of St. Paul), nor 'spurious' (meaning the work of a forger), but 'pseudonymous' (meaning the work of one who made no secret of the fact that he was writing under an assumed name), like so many ancient books, including some of the most precious and most truly inspired in the New Testament itself. Their author's purpose was not to mislead, but to convey as true an account as possible of the Apostle's teaching in its relevance to the needs and conditions of the Sub-Apostolic Age. In welcoming these Epistles his contemporaries showed neither gullibility nor complicity in a fraud, but their ability to recognize a very fine and religiously valuable piece of work, when they saw it.

Much has happened since Bishop A. C. Hervey could write, 'We must remember that, if these Epistles are not St. Paul's, they are artful forgeries, written for the express purpose of deceiving, . . . with a pen steeped in lies and falsehood . . . by some unknown fraudulent impostor', (The Pulpit Commentary, edd. Spence and Exell, London, 1887, pp. ii. v). Today most scholars recognize that there is this third alternative. See Moffatt, *H.N.T.* p. 622 ff.

Commenting on my view that certain genuine notes written

14

by the Apostle Paul to his helpers Timothy and Titus, are
embodied in 2 Timothy and Titus, Spicq wrote 'On revient
ainsi aux pires procédés de la Bible «arc-en-ciel», à une
époque où l'Église, si soucieuse d' orthodoxie et pleine de
vénération pour les écrits apostoliques, aurait accepté ces
joyaux pauliniens enchâssés par la main d' un faussaire dans
une littérature apocryphe, et canonisé le tout!' (Les Épitres
Pastorales, Paris, 1947, p. lxxvi n. 1).

That I regard the Pastorals as apocryphal literature, and
their author as a forger, simply is not true.

* * *

(7) p. 21, A2. One hundred and thirty words occur in the
Pastorals and in other New Testament books, but not in any
Pauline epistle. Of these 1 Timothy has seventy six, 2
Timothy fifty four, and Titus thirty eight.

* * *

(8) p. 35 after Diagram V (The Missing Particles) *one or
other of which has hitherto appeared on the average nine times per
page of his extant letters – not counting the pseudonymous Ephesians.*

* * *

(9) p. 38 (2. GRAMMATICAL PECULIARITIES)
1. The Optative appears in the Paulines twenty six times, in
the Pastorals three times, and all of these are in Paul's own
Last Letter, 2 Tim. i. 16, 18, iv. 16.

* * *

(10) p. 49 (iii). Some of the Latinisms ($\mu\epsilon\mu\beta\rho\acute{a}\nu a$, $\varphi a\iota\lambda\acute{o}\nu\eta s$)
occur in passages the Pauline authorship of which is not
disputed. The rest are regarded by Holtzmann (*PB.*, pp. 109,
271) as favouring his own view that Rome was the birthplace
of these epistles. But Rome was not the only place where
idioms like $\delta\iota$' $\mathring{\eta}\nu$ $a\iota\tau\acute{\iota}a\nu$ (= quam ob rem), $\chi\acute{a}\rho\iota\nu$ $\mathring{\epsilon}\chi\omega$ (=gratiam
habeo) &c. could and did occur quite naturally in a Greek
composition. So, e.g., Epict. III. 9^1, 5^{10}, Plut. I. 17 F, 849 A,
Vit. Romul. 1.

* * *

(11) p. 52-53. Those who would explain the linguistic
peculiarities of the Pastorals as due to an amanuensis point
out quite clearly that it must have been Luke *if anyone* who
filled this role. So James 1906, p. 154, ' "Only Luke is with

15

me"– stares us on the written page'. It is equally clear that they all take for granted the traditional view, making Paul's 'beloved physician' the author of Luke-Acts. For the sake of the argument we may admit that debatable opinion. But even so, as a real solution of our problem this hypothesis can hardly be said to meet the case. . . . Be that as it may, the long lists of words and phrases in the Pastorals to be found in second-century Greek, but not earlier, can no more be explained as due to Paul's friend and physician than as Paul's own.

★   ★   ★

(12) p. 57[19] 1 Tim. v. 11[1].

★   ★   ★

(13) p. 65 f. *Words found in the LXX.*

Jacquier (1903, p. 363) thinks it important that many of the *Hapax Legomena* are in the LXX and must therefore have been known to Paul. So too Rüegg, 1898, p. 65, and Guthrie, 1955, pp. 11 f., 39 f., 1957, p. 47.

Considering what our author says about these 'sacred writings' in 2 Tim. iii. 15 ff., and their huge vocabulary, the really remarkable thing is that the number of these words to be found in the LXX is not far greater than it is – only seventy two out of 167, or 43·1 per cent – not counting the eight which occur in the genuine 'Last Letter'. (Guthrie makes the total seventy eight by counting four of these, ἀγωγή, ἀναψύχω, βέλτιον, ἀκαίρως – also ἤρεμος and ἀφθορία, which do not appear in Swete's text, being *variant readings* found only in the fifth century Codex A, Esth. i. 13 and Hag. ii. 17, where they misrepresent, each in its own way, the original Hebrew). Paul has in Romans 103 *Hapax Legomena* (Appx. I C1), of which 66, or 64 per cent, are in the LXX.

Of the seventy eight 'Residue' words in Appendix I (not counting ἀκαίρως, μεμβράνα, φαιλόνης and ἀφθορία, for the reasons just given), only 18, or 23 per cent, are in the LXX, whereas of the corresponding fifty five in Romans (C1) 26, or 49 per cent, are in the LXX. Of those eighteen, three, βαθμός, νεόφυτος and ὀρθοτομέω, have quite different meanings there

---

[1] ἐν Κυρίῳ forty one times and in every epistle, *not once in the Pastorals.*

16

from their unique metaphorical sense in the Pastorals, καταστολή is in Is. lxi. 3, ἀποθησαυρίζω in Sir. iii. 4, ἐλεγμός = 'reproof' in Sir. xxi. 6, xxxii. 17, xlviii. 7, πορισμός in Wisd. xiii. 9, xiv. 2 and φιλάγαθος in Wisd. vii. 22, ὑδροποτέω in Dan. i. 12, ἐπανόρθωσις in 1 Macc. 14, 14 and 1 Es. 8, 52, ἀκατάγνωστος in 2 Macc. 4. 47, ἔκδηλος in a Macc. 3. 19, 6. 5, and the remaining six, γυμνασία, ἱεροπρεπής, μάμμη, νομίμως, περφρονέω and φλύαρος, only in the apocryphal 4 Maccabees, 'of uncertain date, possibly as late as the time of Josephus' (Swete, Intr. to the O.T. in Greek, p. 372) – so too late for Paul.

The Pastorals, then, like all the other books of the New Testament (except the brief personal note to Philemon), contain a number of quotations from the LXX, and like most other New Testament books, refer to it as 'Scripture'. So it is not at all surprising to find in their vocabulary many points of contact with these sacred writings. What is rather surprising is the very large number of *Hapax Legomena* (A1) in the Pastorals which do *not* occur in the LXX – 95 out of 167.

Of the *Hapax Legomena* (C1) in Romans, Galatians, 1 and 2 Thessalonians taken together 96 out of 165 *do* occur in the LXX, and sixty nine not – almost exactly the opposite proportions to those in the Pastorals.

So, when the vocabulary of these Epistles is viewed in the light of its contacts with that of the Septuagint, after a check-up in Hatch and Redpath's Concordance, the relevant facts, so far from weakening the case against their Pauline authorship, are seen to strengthen it appreciably.

* * *

(14) 81³²-82¹⁰. In the course of our comparative studies we have found nothing in the vocabulary of the Pastorals to conflict with the opinion that their author wrote during the reigns of Trajan and Hadrian, whereas many facts hitherto unknown have emerged which strongly support that opinion. While we search the New Testament, including Paul's own letters, in vain for many of this author's characteristic expressions, we find most of them in Christian writers of the first three quarters of the second century. A few more, to be listed later, appear to be unique in ancient literature, and a still

smaller number occur in earlier writings, but in a different sense from the one they bear here. To find the rest, all that is necessary, as we shall show in full detail in Chapter III, is to extend our researches to non-Christian writers of the same period.

CHAPTER III

THE RESIDUE

There remain eighty two words in the Pastorals – (marked . in Appendix I, A1) – which are not to be found elsewhere in the New Testament, nor in the Apostolic Fathers, nor in the Apologists.

Three of these are in the Genuine Notes embodied in 2 Timothy, ἀκαίρως, which is found in the Classics, LXX, Philo, Josephus and in second century writers, μεμβράνα and φαιλότης =paenula, which are Latin 'loan-words', such as could perfectly well be used by Paul. One, ἑδραίωμα 1 Tim. iii. 15, occurs in the letter to the churches of Lyons and Vienne (Euseb. *H.E.*, V. i. 17, A.D. 177/8), – exactly contemporary with the Apologists Athenagoras and Melito, – leaving seventy eight found in no Christian writing prior to A.D. 178.

The question which naturally suggests itself at this point is: Are these seventy eight words, or any large proportion of of them, to be found in non-Christian writings of the period A.D. 90-178? This again suggests the larger question: Does the vocabulary of the Pastorals as a whole, but more particularly in its non-Pauline elements, coincide to any large extent with that of Dioscorides (*c.* A.D. 100), Dio Chrysostom, Plutarch (who died A.D. 120), Epictetus and his pupil Arrian (who wrote down his discourses), Appian, Philo Byblius, Lucian, Polyaenus, Galen, Vettius Valens, the Emperor Marcus Aurelius Antoninus, and their contemporaries?

The answer to both these questions is in the affirmative. See Appendix I 'Residue', where it is proved that at least sixty one of these seventy eight words do occur, some of them with great frequency, in books of this period. (On the larger question see below, Chapter IV.)

We are left with seventeen (out of the 305 non-Pauline words in the Pastorals), the occurrence of which in Greek writings of the period to which we have assigned these Epistles, we must admit our inability to demonstrate with chapter and verse.

For eleven of these no exact parallel is known to us either before or during the second century. Five are not found anywhere else in ancient literature; but for each of these unique words we have close cognates in our period. Thus in 1 Tim. vi. 5 διαπαρατριβή=perpetual wrangling, the reading of אAD, is simply a heightened form – coined perhaps by our author himself – of παρατριβή, (Polyaenus, Athenagoras and Athenaeus). Similarly 1 Tim. i. 4 ἐκζήτησις, אA and modern editors, is a strengthened form of ζήτησις (T.R. here, Justin, Melito, Tatian, Plut., Dio Chrys., etc.). The verb ἐκζητέω is so common in the Apostolic Fathers, as well as in the LXX, that our author's use of the noun presents no difficulty. For ἀφιλάγαθος 2 Tim. iii. 3 there is φιλάγαθος in Dio Chrys., Plut., and Vettius Valens, as well as earlier, and a host of words like ἀφιλόκαλος (Plut.), ἀφιλόσοφος (Jus.), ἀφιλοξενία (1 Clem.), while ἀφιλοκαλοκαγαθία is found in a second-century papyrus, P. Oxy. 33, ii. 15. Again, συγκακοπαθέω 2 Tim. ii. 3 is a combination, possibly by our author, of συμπαθέω (Ign., Jus., Plut.) with κακοπαθέω (2 Clem., Dio Chrys., Plut. etc.).

καλοδιδάσκαλος Tit. ii. 3 seems to be unique, but κακοδιδασκαλέω occurs in 2 Clem. and Sextus Empiricus, and κακοδιδασκαλία in Ignatius; also καλοσύμβουλος in Ptolemaeus Mathematicus.

Two more are unique in their spelling, as attested by א and accepted by modern editors, πατρολῴας and μητρολῴας 1 Tim. i. 9. Their T.R. forms πατραλοίας and μητραλοίας occur both in the Classics and in second-century writers.

Four more make their only appearance much later, ἀφθορία Tit. ii. 7 in Themistius (iv A.D.), and in one MS, A (v A.D.) of the LXX, Haggai ii. 7. But the adjectival form of this word, ἄφθορος, is in Justin, Artemidorus and Soranus, or, if the reading ἀδιαφθορία be preferred (T.R. and a correcting hand of א), we have ἀδιάφθορος in Dio Chrys., Plut., Appian and Galen. καταστρηνιάω 1 Tim. v. 11 appears again only in the Pseudo-Ignatian Ep. ad Antioch 11, dated by Lightfoot in the latter half of the fourth century (Ign. and Pol. I², p.

260 f., 273). καυστηριάζω 1 Tim. iv, 2, as spelled by א and most modern editors, appears elsewhere only in Leontius (vii A.D.), and perhaps BGU 952, 4? As a variant reading in Strabo V. 1, 9 (ed. G. Kramer, 1884) it is rejected by the best modern editor, A. Meineke, 1921, who omits the σ. λογομαχέω 2 Tim. ii. 14 occurs elsewhere only in Eustathius (xii A.D.). Its cognate λογομαχία 1 Tim. vi. 4 – and a variant reading Tit. iv. 9 rejected by all editors – appears elsewhere only in Porphyry (iii A.D.) twice, Photius (ix A.D.) and the Latin grammarian Nonius (iv A.D.). But we gather from Photius that Conon (i B.C./i A.D.) used it once, and from Nonius that the Latin poet Varro (i B.C.) took it as the title of a Menippean satire.

Five words occur in extant literature in or before St. Paul's lifetime, but not, so far as we know, in the second century, nor in the third. νεόφυτος is in a fragment from Aristophanes, in Philo and the LXX, and in papyri of the first and third centuries, of a newly planted vine or tree, but nowhere in its metaphorical sense = a new adherent, as in 1 Tim. iii. 6. ὀρθοτομέω, only in the LXX Prov. iii. 6, xi. 5, where it means 'direct one's way' or 'cut a straight path before him'. Only in 2 Tim. ii. 15 has it the meaning 'rightly divide' (A.V.) or 'handle aright' (R.V.) the word of truth, or 'drive a straight furrow' (New English Bible) 'in your proclamation of the truth'. ἐλεγμός too is exclusively in the LXX, where it has a variety of meanings, but in Sir. xxi, 6, xxxv (xxxii) 17 = 'reproof', as in 2 Tim. iii. 16. ἐπιδιορθόω appears only in a Greek dialect inscription (Hieropytna ii B.C.), in Themistius (iv A.D.), Syrianus (v A.D.), and Tit. i. 5. Finally διδακτικός 1 Tim. iii. 2, 2 Tim. ii. 24 is in Philodemus rhet. (i B.C.) and Philo. We know that the author of the Pastorals had studied the LXX, for he quotes it 1 Tim. v. 18 f., (2 Tim. ii. 19? cf. W. Lock ad loc.), Tit. ii. 14, and refers to it 2 Tim. iii. 8, 15. It seems highly probable that he had read Philo, for he shares with that writer an exceptionally large number of non-Pauline words (165) and phrases (see below, Appendix II E). That St. Paul had read Philo seems quite improbable and, so far as I know, has never been maintained.

The combined weight of these five words, as telling in

21

favour of the Pauline authorship of these Epistles, is surely negligible[1]. It is certainly far outweighed by the following facts.

(1) Ten of these 'Residue' words appear in non-Christian writers of our period, some of them several times in the same writer, but not, so far as we can discover, in any writing before A.D. 90. ἀνεπαίσχυντος is in Josephus's Antiquities (A.D. 93), also in Agapetus (vi A.D.), ἀντίλυτρον in Zenobius and Polyaenus, also in Orphica Lithica='antidote', and in Kosmas and Damian (dates unknown), in Origen's Hexapla, Ps. 48 (49), 9, Hesychius (v A.D.) and an eighth century papyrus. γάγγραινα is in Dioscorides, Soranus and Galen, (also Hippocrates, but in a passage of very dubious authenticity). In Plut. II 65D it is used figuratively, as in 2 Tim. ii. 17. εὐμετάδοτος occurs twice in M. Aurelius Antoninus and eight times in Vettius Valens, (also once in the 'Vita Aesopi' prefixed by the fourteenth century monk Maximus Planudes to a book of fables supposed to be Aesop's but proved by Bentley to be spurious). θεόπνευστος is in Plutarch and Vettius Valens, (also in that fifth book of the Sibylline Oracles which Blass described as a 'conglomeration' of elements containing clear allusions in oracular form to various historical events and personalities, but with sheer disregard for chronological order – Hadrian and his successors, Nero and his expected return, Vespasian and the destruction of the Temple at Jerusalem (Kautzsch, Dis Pseudepigraphen des Alten Testaments, Tüb., 1900). κενοφωνία is in Dioscorides, Porphyry, Hesychius and Suidas (x A.D.), ξενοδοχέω in Ps-Lucian, 'Amor.', Phrynichus, Maximus Tyrius and Moeris, (late Hellenistic for the classical ξενοδοκέω. In old copies of the Poetae scenici Graeci, ed. Dindorf, 1851, Euripides Alcestis 552 we find τολμᾷς ξενοδοχεῖν; but in the new Liddell and Scott this is quoted with a κ from Gilbert Murray's Euripides). οἰκουργός Tit. ii. 5 ℵ*ACD* &c., edd., (for the

---

[1] ἀγαθοεργέω 1 Tim. vi. 18, Pythag. Ep. 10 (vi B.C.) is not a sixth word in this class. For ἀγαθουργέω. Acts xiv. 7 is an equally correct alternative way of writing this same word–like ἀγαθόεργος Polemo physiogn. I xvi. p. 266, ἀγαθοῦργος Plut. II 307 E, 1015 E.

classical οἰκουρός of T.R.) is in Soranus, πρόκριμα in two ii A.D. papyri and an inscription dated Sparta ii A.D., ὑψηλοφρονέω in Pollux, (also in the T.R. Rom. xi. 20 where, however, אP⁴⁶ &c. read μὴ ὑψηλὰ φρονεῖ, and so modern editors).

(2) To these must be added eight more words, of which the first six occur in the Apostolic Fathers or Apologists, five of them also in non-Christian writings of the same period, but not earlier. δίλογος is in Polycarp (and in Pollux='reiterating', διώκτης is in Barnabas, and the Didache, also Symmachus, Hos. vi. 8? (not in Hatch and Redpath, but see W. Bauer's Wörterbuch s.v.). ἐπισωρεύω is in Barnabas, Plutarch, Epictetus, Artemas Daldianus, Nichomachus, Vettius Valens, Symmachus Hos. xiv. 17, Cant. ii. 4, ἑτεροδιδασκαλέω in Ignatius, ἤρεμος in Athenagoras (cit. 1 Tim. ii. 2), Zenobius, Lucian and two inscriptions ii/iii A.D. (The var lect. in the fifth century codex A LXX Esther iii. 13b, for the ἥμερος of other MSS, is clearly a slip). πρεσβυτέριον in Ignatius=Christian presbytery, as in 1 Tim. iv. 14, (in Lk-Acts of the Jewish assembly or estate of Elders, in Theodotion Susannah 50=honour or privilege of an Elder). A seventh word in this class is ἑδραίωμα, which occurs in the letter of the churches of Lyons and Vienne (see above, p. 19), an eighth, νομοδιδάσκαλος =a doctor of the Law, in Lk. v. 17, Acts v. 34 (both written long after Paul was dead), still an authorized exponent of the Mosaic Law, in 1 Tim. i. 7 a professing Christian who would fain be recognized as a competent interpreter of the Scriptures.

(3) It may help us to appreciate the significance of these facts, if we compare them with the corresponding facts for Paul's own Epistle to the Romans.

Of the 228 words (including *103 Hapax Legomena) found in Romans (Appendix I. C1, C2) but not elsewhere in the ten Paulines, nor in the Pastorals, one is unique, προαιτιάομαι iii. 9; one occurs only in Suidas (x A.D.), ἐπιποθία xv. 25; two in second-century writers but not, so far as we know, earlier, κατάλαλος i, 30='backbiter' is in Hermas and a papyrus of unknown date, but the verb-έω is in Polybius, and the noun -ία in LXX Wisd. and in Paul's own 2 Cor. xii. 20. ἀμετανόητος

23

ii, 5='impenitent', i.e. active in bad sense, appears in Epictetus Fragm. xxv (71), but passive in good sense='not needing repentance'. Otherwise in the second century it= ἀμεταμέλητος 'not to be repented of', i.e. passive in good sense. So Lucian Abd. 11, Vettius Valens 263. 16, Plotinus (iii A.D.).

Of the remaining 224 (*99) *every one* occurs in pagan or Jewish writings, or in both, in or before Paul's lifetime. As was to be expected, most of these occur also in second-century Greek, but not, so far as I can discover, any of the following thirteen words: ἀγριέλαιος, ἀλάλητος, ἀντιστρατεύομαι, ἀνόμως, ἐγγύτερον (adverb), ἑκατονταετής, θήρα, καλλιέλαιος, κατάνυσις c, παλαιότης, συμπαρακαλέω, τολμηρότερον xv. 15 ℵCDG and now P⁴⁶ Chr., Theodor.-Mops., Cyr., al., Souter, von Soden, S. & H. (all supporting T.R. against the unique τολμηροτέρως of A. B. Apollin., W. H. Nestle), also in Thuc, and Polyb., and finally ὑπόδικος.

Thus on purely lexical grounds a date in the first century and indeed during Paul's lifetime, is as clearly indicated for Romans[1] as a date in the second century is for the Pastorals.

This last series of facts – (1), (2) and (3) – had not yet emerged in 1921. So, commenting on our proof that most of the *Hapax Legomena* in these Epistles occur either in the Apostolic Fathers or in the Apologists or in non-Christian writers of the same period, Lock could say 'there is no evidence that the words are not earlier than the second century . . . There is no word impossible to St. Paul, no word not natural to him' (The Pastoral Epistles, 1924, p. xxix).

It was of course never our contention that all, or even most, of these words belong *exclusively* to the second century. Many of them do occur also in Paul's day, or earlier still.

The vocabulary of any generation is always to a very large extent the same as that of its parents and grandparents. The number of fresh words that come into use in the course of fifty or sixty years is comparatively quite small. A still smaller number is apt to drop out of use, and may eventually become obsolete. Others again remain in use, but with a changed meaning. But it is precisely in these few that the difference

[1]On the interpolation i. 19-ii. 1 see below, Chapter VIII.

between the vocabulary of one generation and that of the next or next but one, consists.

In so far, therefore, as Lock's comment refers to a large majority of the words in question, it is an understatement. For there is abundant evidence that they are earlier. But in so far as it refers to the small but crucial minority, it can no longer be said that there is no evidence. The fact that neither the new Liddell and Scott nor Walter Bauer in the latest edition of his great Wörterbuch zum Neuen Testament gives any instance of any one of these words before A.D. 90, may not constitute absolute proof, but it does create a strong presumption against their earlier occurrence in extant literature.

While these authorities do not profess – nor can they be expected – to give all the known cases of a word's occurrence, unless it is a very rare one, they do normally give either the earliest example of its use known to them or at least the name of the earliest writer they know to have used it. The possibility that editors of both these standard works, and their numerous highly competent helpers, have overlooked the occurrence of all these particular eighteen words in the extant writings of St. Paul's or an earlier day must be extremely remote.

Just one more theoretical possibility remains. Some hitherto unknown or long lost work, or some ancient inscription or papyrus, might yet be discovered, proved to belong to Paul's lifetime or an earlier period, and found to contain one or more of our missing words. If and when such a discovery is announced, we should of course modify accordingly our case against the Pauline authorship of the Pastorals. But the probability that all or most of these words will someday have the date of their first known appearance pushed back in this way thirty, sixty or a hundred years or more, must indeed be small. Meanwhile no word can reasonably be called either 'possible' or 'natural' to Paul which, so far as is known, did not come into use till long after he was dead.

CHAPTER IV

NON-PAULINE WORDS IN NON-CHRISTIAN WRITERS, A.D. 90 - 178

In the same literature our 'A' words generally – (A1) *Hapax Legomena* and (A2) non-Pauline words found elsewhere in the New Testament – appear, we might almost say, on every page. It is no uncommon thing to find several of them in a single sentence. Many recur in a dozen or more writers of our period, and a still larger number in half a dozen or more. The total number of occurrences, including repetitions, for which we now have precise reference, runs into thousands – far too many to print. But the main facts can always be verified with the help first of L. & S. and of W. Bauer's Wörterbuch, then of the Indices available in D. Wittenbach, *Plutarchi Index Graecitatis*, Oxon. 1830, H. Schenkl, *Epicteti Dissertationes*, Lips. (T) 1913, M. Antonii Imp. *In semet ipsum Lib. xii*, Lips. (T) 1913, C. C. Reitzius, *Index verborum ac phrasium Luciani*, Trajecti ad Rhenum, 1746, G. Kroll, *Vettii Valentis Anthologiarum Libri* Berlin, 1908, R. Hercherus, *Artemidori Daldiani Onirocriticon Libri V*, Lips. 1864, R. Schneider & G. Uhlig, *Apollonii Dyscoli quae supersunt*, Lips. 1878, 1910; finally by first-hand study of second-century Greek writings to which there is no Index.

Against Philo's 165 non-Pauline words shared with the Pastorals, Lucian has 183, Dio Chrysostom 140, Epictetus 130, M. Aurelius Antoninus 90, all in very much smaller compass, while Plutarch has 217, including *109 *Hapax Leg.*, Appian has 108, Artemidorus 68, Vettius Valens 64, Apollonius Dyscolus 63, Zenobius 62, Aelius Aristides 52, Polyaenus 50, Diogenianus 49, Nichomachus Gerasenus 49, Arrian 46.

The total number found in one or more writers of this period is 270, that is all 305 except the twelve listed above as found in neither period, the five listed as found in writings of Paul's day or earlier, but not after A.D. 90, and not counting the eighteen found in the Genuine Notes embodied in 2 Timothy and Titus.

Of the same 287 words the great majority occur, as was to be expected, in or before Paul's day. The total number is 257, that is all except the twelve found in neither period and eighteen found in our period but not earlier. Two hundred and fifty three are in both periods.

Here then are two periods, the earlier covering all the centuries from Homer to A.D. 90, the later less than one century, between A.D. 90 and 178. The earlier is represented by (a) the whole of our classical Greek literature, (b) post-classical writers of Hellenistic Greek before the Christian era, (c) contemporaries of our Apostle like Strabo and Philo, (d) the whole of the Septuagint, (e) inscriptions and papyri before A.D. 90.

With this very large body of writings we now compare the very much smaller body of those who were on our hypothesis roughly contemporary with the Pastorals, and so arrive at the highly significant result: – while the Pastorals share with writers of both periods 253 words not to be found in any Pauline, we have found in writings of the later period *thirteen more than in (a), (b), (c), (d) and (e) put together.*

Incidentally these facts seem to dispose once and for all of the idea that peculiarities of diction in the Pastorals as compared with the Paulines can be accounted for by referring them to the new subject-matter (PPE p. 50). The subject-matter of these second century writers differs far more widely from that of our author than his subject-matter differs from that of the Paulines. Roman History, Natural History, Medicine, Astrology, Memoirs, Orations on many topics, the interpretation of dreams, collections of proverbs, the Anabasis and death of Alexander, Mathematical problems, Stoic philosophy – there is no end to the variety of themes. Yet every one of these writers shares with the Pastorals a considerable number of words that do not occur in any Pauline.

The total bulk of these writings is much larger than that of the Paulines, or even of the whole New Testament. Let us then take 105 pages comprising the first five orations of Trajan's friend Dio Chrysostom in de Budé's edition. Here

27

we find eighty-three different words occurring with repetitions 322 times, not one of which appears in the 105 pages of our ten Paulines, but all part of the vocabulary of the Pastorals.

All this is just what we might reasonably expect if we knew for certain that these three Epistles were written under Trajan and Hadrian. It seems quite inexplicable if we assume their Pauline authorship either with or without the help of an amanuensis.

CHAPTER V

PHRASES IN THE PASTORALS AND IN SECOND-CENTURY GREEK

In 'The Problem of the Pastoral Epistles' a page of Appendix I was devoted to phrases shared by these Epistles with second-century non-Christian writers. But attention was not otherwise drawn to them or to their significance as indications of the period within which they were written.

In 1948, reviewing Spicq, *Les Épitres Pastorales* in The Journal of Theological Studies, XLIX, p. 208, I wrote 'Words have a long life, but current phrases have a much shorter vogue. A few such as "going off the deep end", "getting the wind up", and "being up against it", would create serious doubts about any document purporting to have been written *c.* A.D. 1863 – 67,' and gave a few cases in point.

In *The Expository Times*, December 1955, after quoting that review, I submitted fourteen examples of this characteristic feature in our author's style. A still larger selection is now given in Appendix II F.

Like many another moralist ancient and modern, St. Paul was apt to use figures of speech from the running-track to illustrate his teaching about the race of life. So 1 Cor. ix. 24-6, Gal. v. 7, Phil. ii. 16, iii. 14 and in his Last Letter embodied in 2 Tim. iv. 7. The author of the Pastorals follows his hero's example in this respect, but in doing so adopts a cliché, $\nu o\mu i\mu\omega s$ $\dot{a}\theta\lambda\epsilon\hat{\iota}\nu =$ '*Play the game*', 2 Tim. iv. 5 not to be found in any Pauline nor, so far as I know, in any other first century writing, but certainly current in our period, for it occurs both in Epictetus and in Galen. So $\pi\rho o\kappa\acute{o}\pi\tau\epsilon\iota\nu$ $\dot{\epsilon}\pi\grave{\iota}$ $\tau\grave{o}$ $\chi\epsilon\hat{\iota}\rho o\nu =$ 'go from bad to worse' 2 Tim. iii. 13 appears twice in Josephus and once in Zenobius, who in Hadrian's day collected popular proverbs, which could be any age, but added their equivalents in the current speech of his day. It is among these last that we find 'those who go from bad to worse'.

29

From the fact that more than a couple of dozen such phrases and word-combinations in the Pastorals can be paralleled from second-century writers – especially their exact contemporaries on our hypothesis, Dio Chrysostom, Epictetus, Plutarch and Zenobius – it is difficult to resist the conclusion that in his phraseology, no less than in his vocabulary, when he is not consciously echoing St. Paul, their author falls naturally and inevitably into the language of his own day.

CHAPTER VI

THE AUTHOR OF EPHESIANS

In this chapter and the next, either of which is incomplete without the other, reasons are given for believing that Onesimus, once the slave of Philemon at Colossae, (1) played a leading part in the collection at Ephesus *c.* A.D. 90 of letters written by St. Paul to his churches, (2) wrote, as an introduction to these and a help towards the better understanding of their message, the inspired summary of St. Paul's teaching which we call Ephesians but he called Laodiceans, and at the same time (3) inserted into Paul's letter to the church at Colossae interpolations designed to meet the needs and guard against the dangers of that subapostolic age, as he was sure Paul would have wished him to do.

I

On the question whether St. Paul was or was not the author of Ephesians, New Testament scholars have been divided since long before anyone now living was born. In that sense it is still one of those great 'open' questions on which experts disagree. On the one hand Josef Schmid[1] and Ernst Percy[2] present an array of facts and arguments in support of the Pauline authorship which to them, and no doubt to many of their readers, seem conclusive. On the other hand Edgar J. Goodspeed[3], John Knox[4], C. L. Mitton[5], Charles Masson[6],

---

[1]*Der Epheserbrief des Apostels Paulus*, Freiburg im B., 1928.

[2]*Die Probleme des Kolosser- und Epheserbriefe*, Lund, 1946.

[3]*New Solutions of New Testament Problems*, Chicago, 1927.
   The Meaning of Ephesians, Chicago, 1933.
   The Key to Ephesians, Chicago, 1956.

[4]*Philemon Among the Letters of Paul*, Chicago, 1933, Revised Edition, New York–Nashville, 1959 and in Great Britain, Collins, 1960.

[5]*The Epistle to the Ephesians*, Oxford, 1951.

[6]*L'Épitre de Saint Paul aux Colossiens*, Neuchâtel, 1950.
   L'Épitre de Saint Paul aux Ephesians, Neuchâtel, 1953.

and Francis W. Beare[1] give reasons which have convinced them and many others that Eph. was written years after St. Paul was dead. Between those who affirm and those who deny the Pauline authorship Dr. H. J. Cadbury, in his Presidential Address on The Dilemma of Ephesians[2], is severely non-committal. 'Readers who expect an attempted proof of one side or the other will not find it here.' (Op. cit. p. 91). In his view we do not know nearly enough about the ways in which the mind of Paul or any other ancient author worked, to determine which is the more likely – that an inventor with the other Paulines before him would succeed in writing a letter which resembles them to the very great extent that Ephesians does, or that Paul himself would write a letter which differs from his other letters to the comparatively small extent that this one does. 'In this obscure area of psychological probability in authorship the problem of the origin of Ephesians ultimately lies' (Op. cit. p. 92). 'Acknowledge as one must the likeness and the difference between Ephesians and the others, we are confronted with an imponderable comparison' (p. 101).

There is no doubt much to be said for Cadbury's argument here. If modern scientists are able to calculate with mathematical precision the place in the sky where a star appeared, or will appear, at a given moment in any night past or future, this is because the star has no will of its own, but is subject to natural laws which cannot be broken. Psychology does not enter as a disturbing element into the astronomer's calculations. But the author of a book or writer of a letter – though he too has his limitations – has a will of his own and a mind of his own, and he can change his mind from time to time. Different minds react differently to the same circumstances, and respond in different ways to the same arguments. The most enlightened minds are the most open to receive new light. There is so much that even the most intimate friends do not know about one another. How can we, after so many

---

[1]*Ephesians, in The Interpreter's Bible*, Vol. X, New York–Nashville, 1955.
Colossians, in The Interpreter's Bible, Vol. XI, New York–Nashville, 1955.
[2]*New Testament Studies*, Vol. 5, No. 2, Cambridge, January 1959.

centuries, be sure what a man like Paul, or a man like Onesimus, would or would not have written at some time in his life?

But while it is all to the good that we should fully realize the inherent difficulties of our problem, and that we should be on our guard against hasty judgements and undue self-confidence, serious students of this problem do not by any means all of them agree that the evidence now available, when taken as a whole, is inconclusive, or that the arguments hitherto put forward by the two sides cancel each other out. On the contrary, there is now a considerable body of scholars who, notwithstanding all that has been or can be said on the other side, have long been convinced that Ephesians is not by Paul. According to Cadbury some scholars 'may feel the strength of the arguments on either side, but are ashamed to make no choice. So they answer the question one way or the other, more because of their unwillingness to admit indecision than out of clear conviction' (Op. cit. p. 93).

But when a man who has devoted much time and thought to the study of this problem, and done his best to estimate fairly the arguments for and against authenticity, comes down in the end on one side or the other, surely the rest of us, whether we agree with his conclusion or not, should give him credit for knowing his own mind and for telling us truthfully what he now believes.

So, while many are on their own showing, like Cadbury himself, still unable to make up their minds, and are apparently waiting for some fresh evidence, or some better statement of the case, to settle the matter for them one way or the other, others who once accepted the traditional opinion have long been fully persuaded that that was a mistake.

This is not due to any failure on their part to appreciate either the inspiration of this Epistle or its many unmistakably Pauline features. Critics who doubt or deny its apostolic authorship still regard it as one of the most precious and most truly inspired books in the New Testament. They agree with Moffatt that it is the work of 'a master hand' (I.L.N.T. 1911, p. 375), and with Eric Graham that it is 'in any case the crown of the Pauline writings' (in A New Commentary on Holy

Scripture, 1928, p. 538). In this respect New Testament scholarship shows a notable advance within living memory.

Sixty six years ago, when some of us were beginning to study this question, the latest standard work on the subject was T. K. Abbott's *Ephesians and Colossians* in The International Critical Commentary (Edinburgh, 1897). There we were told, 'the Epistle makes a distinct claim to be the work of St. Paul – so that, if not genuine, it is the work of a writer who designed that it should be mistaken for the work of that apostle' (p. xvi), and again (referring to H. J. Holtzmann and his theory about Colossians), 'the only value of this part of his work is that it establishes the inadequacy of the more commonly accepted solution of the problem, namely, that Ephesians is simply a forgery based on Colossians, (p. xxiv). So Abbott agreed on one point with those who regarded Ephesians as a forgery – that if not genuine, this Epistle must be the work of a writer whose deliberate intention was to deceive his readers. In drawing this inference, he and they alike were of course utterly and hopelessly wrong, and so is anyone else who argues in the same way. For, in the first place, the very idea that this inspired and inspiring document could be the work of an impostor, who purposed to deceive his readers by passing off his own fabrication as the work of the Apostle, is obviously absurd. In the second place, whoever argues as they did shows that he has completely overlooked the possibility that he who assumed Paul's name – so far from wishing or intending to deceive anybody – made it perfectly clear to his friends, when he showed them his work, and invited them to read it, that he had written it himself; and they in welcoming it, as they certainly did, showed not that they had been craftily deceived, nor that they were consenting parties to a fraud, nor that they had failed to ask him the obvious, natural and proper questions, but that they were capable of recognizing a wonderful interpretation of Paul's teaching when they saw it.

Today nobody believes that Ephesians is a forgery. Certainly neither Goodspeed nor Knox nor Mitton nor Masson nor Beare ever said any such thing. What they do maintain, each in his own way, is that it is the work of one who made no secret of the fact that he wrote in Paul's name what he sincerely believed Paul might have written if he had lived a quarter-century or so longer. In a word used several times in this sense by Mitton – and in this sense only a fair description of what they all have in common – Ephesians is pseudonymous. The mistaken idea that Paul wrote this Epistle himself arose later, just as the idea that he wrote the Pastorals did, when their real author was no longer there to correct it. Whether they themselves accept the Pauline authorship of this Epistle or deny it, scholars no longer regard 'forgery' as the only alternative to authenticity, or even as a possible alternative. Nor do they impute to those who differ from them the opinion that Ephesians is spurious. Nobody now imagines that his own case can be strengthened by attributing such an absurd opinion to his opponents.

The issue today is still between two, and only two, alternatives. If not genuine, Ephesians is the work of one who in perfect good faith, and with no intent or attempt to deceive, set out long after Paul was dead to provide the truest statement he could of Paul's Gospel, in which he himself believed wholeheartedly, and the best summary he could of the main features in Paul's teaching. As Dr. G. B. Caird puts it in his book on *The Apostolic Age* (London, 1955, 1958, p. 133), 'Ephesians . . . if it is not by Paul, is a masterly summary of Paul's theology by a disciple who was capable of thinking Paul's thoughts after him.' To this I would venture to add, Here and there it seems to me that he knew how to put into words, and so make explicit, thoughts which are implicit in Paul's other letters, but nowhere else so explicit as here. So the author of Ephesians, if not St. Paul, must have been a loyal friend and disciple of his, who wrote pseudonymously in the very best sense of that word. This last point needs to be stressed in order to correct the serious misunderstanding that is bound to arise whenever in this connexion the word 'pseudonymous' is taken as meaning 'false' or 'spurious'. So H. J. Cadbury himself, who in his Presidential Address has done so much to clarify the issue, seems inadvertently to confuse it here. For on p. 95 of that Address he writes as if the words 'pseudonymous' and 'spurious' both meant the same

35

thing. 'In dealing with the pseudonymous origin of Ephesians both sides are handicapped by the absence from Christian antiquity of cases where we can compare the spurious with the genuine writings of the same author. . . . What we need for comparison with the problem of Ephesians is cases where we can compare the undoubtedly genuine with the undoubtedly spurious works of an identifiable author.' Such a case would be the apocryphal Epistle to the Laodiceans, (on which see Lft., Col.-Phmn., 1892, pp. 279-298), if we had it in the original Greek. But surely what a spurious Pauline would be like has little or nothing to do with the problem before us. What might well help us by way of comparison would much rather be some cases of 'Pauline' Epistles which are certainly pseudonymous in the same sense as Mitton and the rest believe Ephesians to be pseudonymous.

That we have three such cases ready to hand in the Epistles to Timothy and Titus I am now more firmly convinced than ever, for reasons given earlier in this volume. How far others will find this new evidence convincing remains to be seen. Meanwhile a comparison of these three with Ephesians may prove both interesting and instructive.

Being on our hypothesis more than twenty years later than Ephesians, their vocabulary naturally includes a larger proportion of *Hapax Legomena*, and also of other non-Pauline words and phrases, some of which demonstrably make their first appearance otherwise in the second century. Their author's style is as different from the style of the author of Ephesians as the style of both these writers is from that of Paul. But in his certainly unconscious and unintentional disuse of Pauline particles and prepositions the author of Ephesians comes much nearer to the author of the Pastorals than Paul ever does. (On the special significance of such obviously unconscious symptoms see my comments in *P.P.E.*, p. 58 f., and Cadbury, Op. cit. p. 98.) Nearest to him in this respect we find 2 Thessalonians, and then Colossians (see Diagram V and the lists on pp. 35-37 of P.P.E.). The Pastorals show the same abundance of phrases identical with, or closely resembling, phrases in each of the earlier Paulines, and in addition to these, from Ephesians and 2 Thessalonians. But though they certainly include parallels from Colossians and Philemon, these are not more numerous, nor in any way more striking, than their parallels with other Paulines – whereas in Ephesians the parallels with these two are much more striking than those with any other Pauline, and in number they very nearly equal those with all the other Paulines put together. (See Mitton, *Ephesians*, p. 106). The significance of this is surely obvious. It is exactly what we should expect if our author was, as Knox and Goodspeed maintain, one who knew best of all, and prized most of all, the two letters which Paul had written so long ago for the express purpose of securing his liberation from slavery. For if, as I firmly believe, they are right, and Onesimus was indeed the author of Ephesians, he had the priceless advantage of having known the real Paul intimately in the days of his own impressionable youth. No wonder he shows a deeper understanding of Paul's mind and heart than anyone could match who knew the Apostle only through his letters plus the story in Acts and reports available in Trajan's time. On the other hand, the author of the Pastorals certainly made the most of his own unique advantage, in having access to those three genuine notes, into which Paul had put so much of himself. By embodying these word for word in 2 Timothy and Titus, he preserved them for all time, so that in them we have before us no imitation, however good, but the authentic mind and heart of Paul, as conveyed in his own words to two of his most intimate friends and helpers.

Between these two alternatives, then – Paul himself or a disciple who revered his memory, and was second to none as an exponent of Paul's Gospel – it is for each of us to make his own choice as best he can, bearing in mind that one of these two opinions must be true and the other false, no matter how great the names, or how plausible the arguments, supporting it. For it is quite certain – and nothing could be more so – that one of our two parties has made, and is still persisting in, a very big mistake, due to a serious error of judgement. There is no room for compromise here. *A priori* it seems unlikely that after all these years, in which so many of the world's best scholars have devoted so much time and effort to their search for the truth of this matter, the net result would be a body of evidence which, taken as a whole, points impartially in two opposite directions. Since to err is human, it is surely much more likely that, somewhere in the argument by which exponents of one solution have convinced themselves and others, there is a flaw which has escaped their notice hitherto, but must sooner or later be brought to light. 'Truth will out,' and must in the end prevail. It will then be realized that the facts already known, when taken as a whole and viewed in the right light, are consistent with one solution but quite irreconcilable with the other.

II

But why should anyone doubt that Paul wrote Ephesians? Of many reasons that have been given, here are four which to my mind seem conclusive.

(1) Because – like the Pastorals in this, though far superior to them in other respects – it is too Pauline to be Paul's. One of the chief counts against the Pauline authorship of the Pastorals is the fact that they have far too many phrases taken from far too many of the genuine Paulines. Each of the three has several such composite verbal links with each of the ten. As I wrote forty two years ago (*P.P.E.*' p. 89), 'It is true that Paul himself has, like most other writers, his own favourite turns of speech which keep cropping up in one epistle after another. But we have not found between any one genuine epistle and the others anything like the great series of such composite links connecting the Pastorals with them all.' I cannot see Paul consciously and systematically repeating himself to this extent even in an encyclical, taking care that every one of his other letters was represented by several phrases borrowed from it in this one. Nor is it credible that such a thing would happen just by accident. The first step in my own progress from the one opinion to the other was my discovery in the early nineteen-twenties, after several years of intensive research – long before Goodspeed and Mitton made the facts generally available – that Ephesians, and it alone among the ten Paulines, has a great series of these composite verbal links connecting it chiefly with Colossians, but also with every one

of the other nine Paulines, except 2 Thessalonians. In the case of 2 Thessalonians the resemblances claimed by Goodspeed seem to lack cogency. (See Mitton, *Eph*. p. 246 and his Appendix I.) As the authenticity of this Epistle is open to much more serious doubt than that of 1 Thessalonians, it is all the more in need of such support as it would receive if it could be proved that the author of Ephesians knew and used it in A.D. 90. Once it is admitted that he knew and used all the others, but not this Epistle, the case against it must seem stronger than ever.

Many of the parallels noted by Goodspeed in his epoch-making book, *The Meaning of Ephesians*, are shared with more than one Pauline, as is made clear also in Mitton's lists. But the author of Ephesians has also words and phrases which he shares exclusively with each of the eight, as anyone can verify with the help of Moulton and Geden's Concordance. Thus we may note the examples given overleaf, p.40f. (*=nowhere else in the New Testament except verses cited here).

Returning to our contention that Ephesians is too Pauline to be Paul's, the idea that an imitation can be in a way more like its original than the original itself, paradoxical as it is, conveys a truth that no critic can afford to overlook. As Cadbury himself puts it, 'One could regard the letter as in some respects more Pauline than Paul' (Op. cit. p. 99). This too is surely the real point and moral of the amusing story at the end of his Address about the popular schoolmaster whose former pupils engaged in a competition to decide which of them could give the best imitation of "Puddles" reciting a favourite piece of verse. Unknown to the judges "Puddles" himself took part like the rest behind the curtain, with the result that he was awarded the third place – two of his pupils being judged to have done better than he did.

(2) My next step was to reconsider the marked contrast between the syle of Ephesians and that of the other Paulines. This has been admitted by most scholars since Erasmus wrote, 'Certe stylus tantum dissonat a ceteris Pauli epistolis ut alterius videri possit, nisi pectus atque indoles Paulinae mentis hanc prorsus illi vindicaret'. We may well agree that Erasmus

Eph.	Rom.
ii.18 δι' αὐτοῦ ἔχομεν τὴν *προσαγωγὴν	v.2 δι' οὗ καὶ τὴν *προσαγωγὴν ἐσχή-
iii.12 ἐν ᾧ ἔχομεν τὴν ...*προσαγωγὴν	καμεν
i.9 * προέθετο	{ i.13 * προεθέμην
i.11, iii.11 κατὰ πρόθεσιν	{ iii.25 * προέθετο
	{ viii.28 κατὰ πρόθεσιν
	{ cf. i.11 ἡ κατ' ἐκλογὴν πρόθεσις τοῦ Θεοῦ
	(2 Tim. i.9 κατὰ ἰδίαν πρόθεσιν)
ii.10 * προητοίμασεν	ix.23 * προητοίμασεν
iii.6 * συνκληρονόμα	viii.17 (+ Heb. xi.9, 1 Pe. iii.7) * συνκληρονόμοι
iii.8 * ἀνεξιχνίαστον	xi.33 * ἀνεξιχνίαστοι
iv.25 ἐσμὲν ἀλλήλων μέλη	xii.5 ἐσμεν, ... ἀλλήλων μέλη
	1 Cor.
ii.9 ἵνα μή τις καυχήσηται	i.29 ὅπως μὴ καυχήσηται πᾶσα σάρξ
vi.24 ἐν ἀφθαρσίᾳ	xv.42 ἐν ἀφθαρσίᾳ
i.21 #. ὑπεράνω πάσης ἀρχῆς καὶ	xv.24-28 ὅταν καταργήσῃ πᾶσαν ἀρχὴν καὶ
ἐξουσίας καὶ δυνάμεως ...	πᾶσαν ἐξουσίαν καὶ δύναμιν ...
πάντα ὑπέταξεν ὑπὸ τοὺς πόδας	πάντα ... ὑπέταξεν ὑπὸ τοὺς πόδας
αὐτοῦ ... τοῦ τὰ πάντα ἐν πᾶσιν	αὐτοῦ ... ἵνα ᾖ ὁ Θεὸς πάντα ἐν πᾶσιν
πληρωμένου	
v.23 ἀνήρ ἐστιν κεφαλὴ τῆς γυναικὸς	xi.3 παντὸς ἀνδρὸς ἡ κεφαλὴ ὁ Χριστός
ὡς καὶ ὁ Χριστὸς κεφαλὴ τῆς	ἐστιν, κεφαλὴ δὲ γυναικὸς ὁ ἀνὴρ
ἐκκλησίας	**2 Cor.**
i.3 Εὐλογητὸς ὁ Θεὸς καὶ Πατὴρ τοῦ	i.3 Εὐλογητὸς ὁ Θεὸς καὶ Πατὴρ τοῦ
Κυρίου ἡμῶν Ἰησοῦ Χριστοῦ, ὁ	Κυρίου ἡμῶν Ἰησοῦ Χριστοῦ, ὁ
	+ 1 Pe. i.3
ii.3 ἀνεστράφημεν	i.12 ἀνεστράφημεν (+ 1 Tim. iii.15 and
	N.T. passim but not elsewhere in Paul)
i.13 ἐσφραγίσθητε τῷ Πνεύματι ...	{ i.22 ὁ καὶ σφραγισάμενος ἡμᾶς καὶ
τῷ Ἁγίῳ, ὅς ἐστιν *ἀρραβὼν	{ δοὺς τὸν *ἀρραβῶνα τοῦ Πνεύματος
τῆς κληρονομίας ἡμῶν	{ v.5 ὁ δοὺς ἡμῖν τὸν *ἀρραβῶνα
	τοῦ Πνεύματος
ii.4. πλούσιος ὤν	viii.9 πλούσιος ὤν (+ 1 Tim. vi.7 and
	N.T., but not elsewhere in Paul)
	Gal.
i.10 τοῦ πληρώματος τῶν καιρῶν	iv.4 τὸ πλήρωμα τοῦ χρόνου
iii.3 κατὰ ἀποκάλυψιν	i.12 κατὰ ἀποκάλυψιν
v.2 καθὼς καὶ ὁ Χριστὸς ἠγάπησεν	ii.20 τοῦ υἱοῦ τοῦ Θεοῦ τοῦ ἀγαπήσαντός
ἡμᾶς καὶ παρέδωκεν ἑαυτὸν	με καὶ παραδόντος ἑαυτὸν
ὑπὲρ ἡμῶν	ὑπὲρ ἐμοῦ
vi.6 (μὴ ... ὡς ἀνθρωπάρεσκοι, ἀλλ')	i.10 εἰ ἔτι ἀνθρώποις ἤρεσκον,
ὡς δοῦλοι Χριστοῦ (cf. Col. iii.22)	Χριστοῦ δοῦλος οὐκ ἂν ἤμην
iii.8 ἐμοὶ ... ἐδόθη ἡ χάρις αὕτη,	i.15 ὁ ... με ... καλέσας διὰ τῆς χάριτος
τοῖς ἔθνεσιν εὐαγγελίσασθαι	αὐτοῦ ἵνα εὐαγγελίζωμαι αὐτὸν
	ἐν τοῖς ἔθνεσιν

40

<table>
<tr><td valign="top">

Eph.

i.21 ὑπεράνω...παντὸς ὀνόματος ὀνομαζομένου

v.2 θυσίαν τῷ θεῷ εἰς ὀσμὴν εὐωδίας

iii.16 Κατὰ τὸ πλοῦτος τῆς δόξης αὐτοῦ

iii.20f. τῷ δὲ...αὐτῷ ἡ δόξα...εἰς πάσας τὰς γενεὰς τοῦ αἰῶνος τῶν αἰώνων· ἀμήν.

iv.1 Παρακαλῶ...ὑμᾶς...ἀξίως περιπατῆσαι τῆς κλήσεως ἧς ἐκλήθητε

ii.3 ὡς καὶ οἱ λοιποί

ii.12 ἐλπίδα μὴ ἔχοντες

v.9 ὡς τέκνα φωτὸς περιπατεῖτε

iii.1 ἐγὼ Παῦλος ὁ δέσμιος τοῦ Χριστοῦ Ἰησοῦ

iv.1 (Παρακαλῶ...ὑμᾶς) ἐγὼ ὁ δέσμιος ἐν Κυρίῳ

vi.20 ὑπὲρ οὗ πρεσβεύω ἐν ἁλύσει

i.16 μνείαν ποιούμενος ἐπὶ τῶν προσευχῶν μου

</td><td valign="top">

Phil.

ii.9 τὸ ὄνομα τὸ ὑπὲρ πᾶν ὄνομα

iv.18 ὀσμὴν εὐωδίας, θυσίαν δεκτήν, εὐάρεστόν τῷ θεῷ

(Ps. xi.7 θυσίαν καὶ προσφορὰν οὐκ ἠθέλησας, Ps. l.14 θῦσον τῷ θεῷ θυσίαν αἰνέσεως)

iv.19 Κατὰ τὸ πλοῦτος αὐτοῦ ἐν δόξῃ

iv.20 τῷ δὲ θεῷ...ἡ δόξα εἰς τοὺς αἰῶνας τῶν αἰώνων· ἀμήν.

cf. 1 Tim. i.17 τῷ δὲ...δόξα εἰς τοὺς αἰῶνας τῶν αἰώνων· ἀμήν.

2 Tim. iv.18 ᾧ ἡ δόξα εἰς τοὺς αἰῶνας τῶν αἰώνων, ἀμήν.

1 Thess.

ii.12 παρακαλοῦντες ὑμᾶς...εἰς τὸ περιπατεῖν ὑμᾶς ἀξίως τοῦ θεοῦ τοῦ καλοῦντος ὑμᾶς

iv.13 καθὼς καὶ οἱ λοιποὶ οἱ μὴ ἔχοντες ἐλπίδα

v.6 ὡς οἱ λοιποί

v.5 πάντες..ὑμεῖς υἱοὶ φωτός ἐστε

Phmn.

1 Παῦλος δέσμιος Χριστοῦ Ἰησοῦ

10 Παρακαλῶ σε περὶ...

9 Παῦλος πρεσβύτης, νυνὶ δὲ καὶ δέσμιος Χριστοῦ Ἰησοῦ

4f. μνείαν σου ποιούμενος ἐπὶ τῶν προσευχῶν μου

</td></tr>
</table>

showed his usual sound judgement both in his recognition of that constrast and in his appreciation of the way in which Paul's heart and mind are portrayed in this Epistle. The crucial question is, Was he also right in concluding that this last consideration overrides those differences in style and, in spite of them all, establishes the Pauline authorship of Ephesians? Can the opposite conclusion, which Erasmus himself admitted he must otherwise have drawn from those differences, be so easily dismissed? I say 'easily' because Erasmus seems to have made no attempt to explain how Paul came to write this particular Epistle in a style contrasting so sharply with his own, as this appears in his other writings. As the same great scholar wrote in another connexion, 'Non est cujusvis hominis Paulinum pectus effingere'. But he did not say, 'Nemo unquam potuit . . .', and we must not mentally substitute those words for his 'non est cujusvis . . .' To assume that none but Paul could so portray the heart of Paul as this is done in Ephesians would be to beg the whole question now at issue.

Let us then here and now examine the style of Ephesians in detail[1] – first its long, unwieldy sentences, with one subordinate clause, now relatival, now participial, after another, and yet another, in a succession that would be tedious if the subject-matter were not so inspiring, running on and on to fifteen, nineteen, twenty two or twenty four lines in W.H. before they come to a full-stop. Five of these periods (i. 3-14, i. 15-23, ii. 1-7, iii. 1-12, iv. 11-16) make up more than a third of the whole Epistle. Then its unparalleled number of genitival formations, including the coupling of two synonymous nouns with a genitive, its quite un-Pauline superabundance of synonyms which, as Moffatt says, often add little or nothing to the sense, its frequent association of a noun with the cognate verb, its excessive use of the preposition ἐν, to which I would add its almost complete disuse of those numerous Pauline particles and prepositions which are conspicuous by their absence from the Pastorals, and its use of

---

[1]See Moffatt, *I.N.L.T.* p. 387, Mitton, *Eph.* p. 9 ff., Cadbury, Op. cit. p. 98 f.

several such words which do not occur in any Pauline ($\epsilon\delta$, $\mu\alpha\kappa\rho\acute{\alpha}\nu$ 2, $\acute{\upsilon}\pi\epsilon\rho\acute{\alpha}\nu\omega$ 2, $\acute{\alpha}\mu\phi\acute{o}\tau\epsilon\rho\sigma\iota$ 3). Also the curious fact that whereas Romans has ninety two question marks in its twenty six pages, 1 Corinthians 100 in twenty four pages, 2 Corinthians twenty seven in sixteen and three quarter pages, Galatians sixteen in eight and a quarter pages, Ephesians has only one (iv. 9) in eight and three quarter pages of W.H.

As Buffon wrote, 'Le style est l'homme même'. While this man shows by *what he says* that he has much in common with Paul, his *way of saying it* shows that, when he is actually composing a sentence, his mind works in a very different way from Paul's. The best words to express his meaning do not spring to his mind so quickly or so spontaneously as they do to Paul's mind. Here is a man who will often write several lines of a sentence before he has made up his mind how to finish it. That was not Paul's way. Or was it? Can it be claimed, on the strength of two passages in Colossians (i. 9-23, ii. 8-15), which cover thirty three and a half lines and eighteen lines respectively before they come to a full-stop, that Paul himself had this same idiosyncrasy? The answer would clearly be Yes, and this part of our argument would fall to the ground, if we really knew that Paul wrote the whole of Colossians in its present form. But to take that for granted, as many do, is to beg a very important and much disputed question, and to overlook a considerable body of evidence which has never yet been shown to be compatible with such an assumption. For this evidence see below, Chapter VII, where it is pointed out (a) that the style of both these passages is marked not only by the same long-drawn periods as Ephesians but also by all those other features which we have seen to characterize the style of that Epistle, (b) that there is no other passage in Colossians, or in any other Pauline, of which the same can be said, (c) that when Col. ii. 7-iii. 1 is subjected to the same linguistic tests as we have applied to the Pastorals, this passage comes out on a par with 1 Timothy. In face of these facts the traditional opinion, that Paul wrote the whole of Colossians, as it now stands, is surely no longer tenable. So far as I can see, the only hypothesis that meets the case is to the effect that a genuine letter sent by Paul to the church at Colossae was interpolated by the author of Ephesians. Nor am I alone in this. Charles Masson in his L'Épitre de Saint Paul aux Colossiens tells how he was led by an entirely different path to much the same conclusion. Only his interpolations are much more extensive than mine, and his original letter much shorter. I submit that too little attention has yet been given to the possibility that some greatly simplified form of Holtzmann's famous theory may prove to be the final solution of this old problem.

(3) If Paul wrote Ephesians, he can only have done so at the same time and place as his letters to Philemon and the church at Colossae. When and where was this? Tradition says Rome during the imprisonment of Acts xxviii, and defenders of the authenticity from Lightfoot and Zahn[1] to Ernst Percy agree that language and subject-matter alike forbid any earlier date. But Ephesus is now favoured by quite a large body of experts as the birthplace, and *c.* A.D. 55/56 as the date, of Colossians-Philemon, and the case for this is far stronger than Duncan made it[2]. For, while he rightly drew attention to the great difference between a thousand miles by road plus two sea voyages taking at least five days together (another 300 miles), from Colossae to Rome, and the mere 100 from Colossae to Ephesus, it is now clear (a) that Onesimus must have made that journey not once only, but three times. For the first thing Paul did after this youth's conversion was to send him back to his master with a letter which he (Paul) had no doubt whatever would lead its recipient not only to forgive Onesimus but forthwith to grant him his freedom, and then send him back to his father in God, to serve him no longer as a slave, but for love. For the proof that Onesimus was in fact returned as a freedman to serve Paul on his former master's behalf, see John Knox's brilliant essay,

---

[1] Lft., *Col-Phmn.*, 1892, p. 37, 'towards the close of the Apostle's captivity, about the year 63'. *Phil.* 1894, pp. 30-46, 'The facts are best met by placing the Epistles to the Colossians and Ephesians in St. Paul's first Roman captivity'. Zahn, *Einl. N.T.*, 1906, p. 316, „An der Abfassung der drei Briefe in Röm während der zwei Jahre AG. xxviii. 30 ist nicht zu zweifeln".
[2] George S. Duncan, St. Paul's Ephesian Ministry, London, 1929.

Philemon Among the Letters of Paul, Chicago, 1935, now available in a Revised Edition (above, p. 1, n. 4). Also *Onesimus and Philemon* by P. N. Harrison, Anglican Theological Review, October, 1950. (b) When Onesimus made that journey for the second and third times, he did not make it alone. With him went Tychicus who, having carried out his instructions, would naturally return to Ephesus, where he belonged (Acts, xx. 4, xxi. 29). (c) Paul himself was to follow very soon. Whether he was in fact able, when the time came, to pay that visit, is not recorded, but such was certainly his intention. He would then return to Ephesus, before proceeding elsewhere. (d) Yet another visitor to Colossae, now with Paul, to be expected soon, is Mark (iv. 10). If Paul was in Rome, the total distance of all these journeys to and fro adds up to 8,100 miles, compared with 900 if he was at Ephesus. According to Ernst Percy, 'We must bear in mind that ancient men did not reckon the time spent on travel by the same standards as we do, and in view of the lively communications which then existed between Rome and Asia Minor, a journey from Rome to Colossae would not be regarded as anything remarkable' (Op. cit. p. 434, Translation mine). But surely this does not meet the case. The idea that Paul the Traveller would not think twice before he committed himself and his companions to a series of journeys totalling more than eight thousand miles, does not seem very plausible to me.

Further, when he was in Rome awaiting his trial before Nero on a capital charge, he was in dire peril of his life, and knew it. But there is no hint in either of these two letters to Colossae that he was in any sort of danger. On the contrary, he confidently expects to be at liberty in the near future, and makes his plans accordingly. So in all probability his present imprisonment is some form of *libera custodia,* such as might well have been imposed by friendly Asiarchs (Acts xix. 31), to keep him out of the way of Jewish fanatics, and avoid a riot. The lack of reference in Acts to a brief incident of this kind is nothing like so great a difficulty as the fact that in Acts there is not only no mention, but no room in the story, for the much more serious imprisonments also postulated by Duncan.

On all these grounds it seems highly improbable that Paul

wrote his letters to Philemon and the church at Colossae as a prisoner in Rome, and practically certain that he did so at Ephesus *c.* A.D. 55/56. But this is, as we have seen, much too early a date for Ephesians, from which it follows that Paul cannot have been the author of this Epistle.

(4) If critics are right in assigning to Ephesians a date *c.* A.D. 90, this is itself of course decisive against Paul's authorship. The reasons for this are three-fold. (i) As Goodspeed showed in his *New Solutions* . . . an earlier date for the first collection of Pauline Epistles at Ephesus, and for the composition of Ephesians, is excluded by the certain fact that no sign can be found in Acts of its author's acquaintance with this or with any Pauline Epistle. For, while his ignorance of the others is fully accounted for by bearing in mind that each of the letters to particular churches would naturally lie hidden away in the strong-box of the church to which it was addressed – since they were obviously not intended for general publication, and Paul's severe remarks chiding the original recipients could never have been shown to a stranger so long as these were alive – 'Luke's' ignorance of Ephesians cannot be explained in the same way, or in any other way, so long as its Pauline authorship is assumed. See further below, p. 53 f.

(ii) It is widely recognized, and particularly well brought out by Charles Masson in his Commentaries on Ephesians and Colossians, that while the author of Ephesians and interpolator of Colossians was a faithful follower of St. Paul, whose voice he wished to make heard in the Church, the disciple is not the master, he is himself, and he belongs to his own time, which is toward the end of the first century. He develops ideas which are latent or implicit in Paul's own letters, drops some doctrines taught explicitly by the Apostle, and introduces others not to be found in the genuine Epistles. In Paul the Church's one foundation is Jesus Christ (1 Cor. iii. 11), in Eph. ii. 20 it is the apostles and prophets, Christ being its cornerstone. The Eschatology so strongly marked in Paul has almost disappeared, while Demonology is much more pronounced, more advanced, and fills a larger place than in the other Paulines.

Dr. G. B. Caird in his *Principalities and Powers* (Oxford,

1956, p. viii) says, 'the idea of sinister world powers and their subjugation by Christ is built into the very fabric of Paul's thought, and some mention of it is found in every epistle except Philemon'. But in this book Caird takes for granted the Pauline authorship both of Ephesians and of Colossians in its present form, referring to these as Paul's 'two later epistles' (pp. 20, 85). Apparently he does not regard the work of scholars like Goodspeed, Knox, Mitton and Masson as worth mentioning. To my mind there is much more in them than he allows. I feel sure that references to those sinister world powers and Christ's victory over them in Ephesians and the interpolated verses in Colossians are much better understood as developments of Paul's thought by his devoted friend and disciple writing more than twenty five years after Paul's death.

The same observations apply to G. H. C. Macgregor's otherwise admirable paper on *Principalities and Powers; the Cosmic Background of Paul's Thought*, in New Testament Studies, Vol. 1, No. 1, Cambridge, Sept. 1954. On p. 21 he writes, "That Paul himself was in bondage to such superstition is not for one moment suggested. But that such was the background of the religious experience of most of his pagan converts can hardly be denied. And that Paul's message to them is deliberately related to that background appears in particular from two of his most important phrases. First in Eph. vi, 12 he speaks of τοὺς κοσμοκράτορας τοῦ σκότους τούτου, 'the world-potentates of this darkness'. . . . Secondly, twice in Galatians and twice in Colossians (Gal. iv. 3, 9; Col. ii. 8, 20) Paul uses the even more suggestive designation στοιχεῖα – three times with the familiar addition, τοῦ κόσμου."

Macgregor takes for granted the Pauline authorship of Ephesians and the whole of Colossians, and assumes a date within Paul's lifetime for the Testament of Solomon, from which the phrase 'world-rulers of this darkness' is taken by the author of Ephesians. He is confident that the word στοιχεῖα in Galatians, no less than in Colossians, means those sinister invisible powers, 'the world-rulers of this darkness' of Ephesians. Does he find no difficulty in Paul's description of these as 'weak and beggarly'? Lightfoot's interpretation of στοιχεῖα here surely makes far better sense. On p. 24 Macgregor quotes Rom. xiii. 1 and Tit. iii. 1 and adds, 'There is of course no question that in both passages Paul is speaking about the secular state'. So in Macgregor's view any question as to the Pauline authorship of the Epistle to Titus simply does not arise.

(iii) Lexical evidence. We could hardly expect so much decisive help in confirming c. A.D. 90 as the date of Ephesians and of our Interpolations in Colossians from a lexical study of their vocabulary, as we have received in fixing Trajan's later years and the beginning of Hadrian's reign for the Pastorals, because (a) the interval between Paul's death and A.D. 90 is so much shorter, and (b) these documents are so brief, while (c) an even larger proportion of Ephesians consists of phrases borrowed from the Paulines.

The number of New Testament *Hapax Legomena* per page in Ephesians is about the same as in other Paulines, forty in eight and three quarter pages, and most of these are in the Classics, so are equally compatible with either date. Two occur only in Ephesians, συναρμολογέω ii. 21 and σύνσωμος ii. 19. Two more words are shared exclusively with our Interpolations in Colossians, ἀποκαταλλάσσω Eph. ii. 12, iv. 18, Col. i. 21 and συνζωοποιέω Eph. ii. 5, Col. ii, 13. ἐλαχιστότερος Eph. iii. 3 (cf. ἐλάχιστος 1 Cor. xv. 9) is unique, but Winer and L. & S. compare ἐλαχιστότατος Sext. Emp. *Adv. Math.* 3.54, 9.406 (ii A.D.). With κλυδωνίζομαι Eph. iv. 14 cf. Joseph. *Ant.* IX. 11, 3 ὁ δῆμος ἅπας ταρασσόμενος καὶ κλυδωνιζόμενος . . . (A.D. 93), Vett. Val. 354²⁶, Is. lvii. 20 LXX. (Our only pre-Christian example of this word – unless Or. Syb. 1. 289 is another?). Aristaen. *EP.* 27 H (v A.D.) is too late to count either way. With μεθοδεία Eph. vi. 11 (since Plato and Xenophon) Bauer compares Dio Chrys. 53 (LXX) 4, also μεθοδεύω=betrügen Epict. II. 19, 28, III. 21. 22. κοσμοκράτορες Eph. vi. 12 Vett. Val. 278², 360⁷, Jamblichus *Myst.* 2³ οἱ κοσμοκράτορες οἱ τὰ ὑπὸ σελήνην στοιχεῖα διοικοῦντες, 2⁹, 3¹⁰ (c. A.D. 300). According to M. Dibelius, *Die Geisterwelt im Glauben des Paulus*, 1909, p. 230, spirits come to Solomon and call themselves οἱ κοσμοκράτορες τοῦ σκότους τούτου. I have not been able to find anyone who can tell me the date of

Testamentum Salomonis. But it seems much more likely that the author of Ephesians is quoting this Jewish book than *vice versa*. Should it prove to have been written after Paul died, this would tell strongly against the traditional opinion.

As references for κυριότητες (Eph. i. 21, Col. i. 16, 2 Pe. ii. 10, Ju. 8) in this new and special sense=angelic powers, Bauer gives Enoch 61, 10 and Slav. Enoch 20. For i A.D. as the date of this part of Enoch see Georg Beer in Kautzsch, *Die . . . Pseudepigraphen des A.T.'s*, Tübingen, 1900, p. 224. For θρόνοι Col. i. 16 plural again=sinister angelic powers, cf. Test. Levi 3. 8, P. Mich. 149 xvi. 23, 24 (iii A.D.). On Test. Levi, F. Schnapp in Kautzsch, *Pseudepigr. d. A.T.* p. 460 says „Die Thatsache darf . . . als festgestellt betrachtet werden, dass wir hier eine ursprünglich jüd. Schrift vor uns haben, die dürch Uberarbeitung für den Gebrauch der christlichen Gemeinde zurechtgemacht ist." As to whether this verse is Jewish original or Christian addition, he does not express an opinion.

I can find nothing in these facts that points away from A.D. 90 and toward a date within Paul's lifetime. On the contrary, it seems to me that the lexical evidence as a whole makes the later date definitely the more probable of the two.

When we come to the corresponding evidence touching our Interpolations in Colossians (Chapter VII), we shall find there too a similar result – a number of words which make their first appearance otherwise about the end of the first century or later.

Any one of these four considerations would seen to raise serious doubts about the Pauline authorship of Ephesians. Their combined effect is surely to make the traditional opinion quite untenable.

III

This being so, Ephesians can only have been written by someone who knew and understood St. Paul as well as, or better than, anyone else has ever done. In this 'great rhapsody on the worth of the Christian salvation', as it has been well called by Goodspeed (*The Meaning of Ephesians*,

p. 3), its author has not only given us what is admittedly the best summary we possess of the main features in Paul's teaching, he has also portrayed the heart of Paul as no one else has ever done. Such knowledge and understanding could not have been acquired by anyone who had never set eyes on him, through studying his letters and reading the story of his life in Acts plus traditions available twenty five years after he died. It could only have been derived from Paul himself by one who had received 'the truth as it is in Jesus' (Eph. iv. 21) from Paul's own lips.

But he did not have to depend entirely on his memory of things he had heard his great teacher say long years ago. He also shows a truly remarkable familiarity with those letters written by Paul which have come down to us. First and foremost he must have known that letter to the church at Colossae almost by heart. For the echoes from this, and from the one to Philemon that went with it, just about equal in number those from all the others put together. But we must not belittle his knowledge of those others, for his borrowings from them prove that he had studied every one of them with reverent care. In these echoes he does not show the cold precision of a mere scribe who mechanically copies out whole sentences from the original before him word for word. But the net result is a wonderful summary of the master themes which constitute Paul's Gospel, minus those purely local and temporal matters which, in each of these letters to particular churches, lead up to the universal truths that give them their value for all Christian readers everywhere. Still our author can, if he wishes, reproduce verbatim a whole passage like the reference to Tychicus – Eph. vi. 21 f. = Col. iv. 7 f. – which suggests that he had a copy, if not the original, of that letter available for use when required.

In assuming the name of his revered teacher, his purpose was, first, to glorify God (i. 6, 12, 14), then to do honour not to himself but to Paul, by setting forth Paul's Gospel in such a way as would best help others to understand and believe it. He took Paul's name, further, because it was indeed Paul's Gospel far more than his own that he was proclaiming. For it was revealed to Paul first-hand by a Light and a Voice direct from heaven, when this writer was still in the darkness of heathenism, dead in sin, and in bondage to evil habits and evil desires, from which Paul under heaven delivered him.

IV

Paul made many converts, and had quite a little company of devoted followers, any one of whom would have been more than glad to do for him anything in his power. But all we have been saying applies to one of them far more clearly, and far more closely, than to any of the others – one whose reason for being interested in any letter that Paul had written, but above all in the one to Philemon and the others that went with it to Laodicea and Colossae, was unique. For he, Onesimus, had actually gone at Paul's bidding with their bearer Tychicus first to Laodicea and then on to Colossae. To him the one to Philemon was in a way the most important that Paul ever wrote. For it was written expressly on his behalf, its occasion was his own conversion, and its purpose was to secure his release from slavery and his return to Paul to look after him as his willing helper, companion and friend. By achieving this purpose it had changed the whole course of his life.

*　　*　　*

Can Onesimus be identified with the Onesiphorus of 2 Tim. i. 16-18, iv. 19, as suggested in my *Onesimus and Philemon?* Absolute certainty on a point of this kind is of course out of the question. But the new chapter this would add to our life of Onesimus – in which he makes for himself such wonderful opportunities for ministering to the Apostle again, and for getting to know him better than ever during those last days of his life – still seems to me highly probable, and is surely at least an intensely interesting possibility. For the formations cf. θανάσιμος (θ. τύχαι, Aeschylus, *Ag.* 1276) and θανατηφόρος Aesch. *Ch.* 369 (θ. αἶσα). Seeing that Prisca and Priscilla are undoubtedly the same person – so are Silas and Silvanus, Saul and Paul, Cephas and Peter – why not Onesimus ('Helpful') and Onesiphorus ('Help-bearing' or '-bearer')? If not, then we are confronted with the very curious coincidence of two different friends and helpers with such very similar names (or similar forms of the same name), rendering many services of the same kind at the same time and place (Ephesus), and yet Paul reminds Timothy only of the one, but is not himself reminded of the other. Had Paul by this time forgotten all about Onesimus and the services by which he had made himself so useful (εὔχρηστον) at Ephesus in the days of his youth? During the years between Paul's departure from Ephesus and his martyrdom, then, Onesimus will have come of age and settled down at Ephesus with a household of his own, growing all the while in grace and in favour with Paul's friends there, especially Prisca and Aquila. During the last two of those years he will have shared to the full their growing anxiety about the prisoner first of Burrus then of Tigellinus (as successive chiefs of the Pretorian Guard). Finally he must needs drop everything and set off on the long journey to Rome, there to repeat again and again (πολλάκις) so long as it was humanly possible, and at no small risk to himself, the sort of ministrations he had rendered years ago at Ephesus, as Timothy knew better (βέλτιον) than most people. But in his zeal to bring all the help and comfort he could to the prisoner, he has ventured once too often into that danger area, and has been arrested, presumably on suspicion of too active sympathies with one now on trial under a capital charge. See my *Problem of the Pastoral Epistles,* pp. 127-30. Of course Paul could not know, when he was writing his Last Letter, that this loyal friend, having put his own life in jeopardy, would after all be delivered from that danger, being acquitted by the authorities of any serious offence against the State – still less that he would live to become the collector of Paul's letters, author of our so-called Epistle to the Ephesians, and eventually bishop of Ephesus – all of which must have belonged to the same life-story, if we are right in regarding Onesiphorus as Paul's own familier variant on the name Onesimus, which Timothy would recognize as such, so would know perfectly well who was meant. It is quite certain that Timothy was in fact familiar with plays like this on the names of Paul's friends. For he was himself joint sender of letters in which they occur –'Ονήσιμον . . . ἄχρηστον . . . εὔχρηστον . . . ὀναίμην, Phmn. 10 f, 20, 'Επαφρόδιτον . . . παραβολευσάμενος

52

Phil. ii. 25, 30. So he can hardly have failed to recognize one of them in a letter of which he was the recipient. For Epaphroditus = Felix ($E\dot{v}\tau v\chi\eta s$), Fortune's favourite, maker of the winning throw at dice (Venus), see Plutarch, *Sulla* xxxiv, Appian, *B.C.* I, 97. For $\pi a\rho a\beta o\lambda\epsilon v\sigma\acute{a}\mu\epsilon vos$ ... = gambling his life, see Lft., *Phil.* ii. 10.

★   ★   ★

Be that as it may, thanks to John Knox and his book about Philemon, the identity of Paul's young convert with the bishop of Ephesus who sixty years later visited Ignatius at Smyrna, when that saintly bishop of Antioch was on his way to Rome and martyrdom, is established beyond reasonable doubt by the amazing series of echoes from Philemon in the letter that Ignatius wrote to the church at Ephesus, extolling their bishop, whose 'well-loved name' was Onesimus. From this it follows that, whether or not Onesimus was already bishop of Ephesus in A.D. 90, he must have been highly respected and very influential there at that time. So that when, as the result of the publication of Acts, Paul's letters were collected there, it is unthinkable that he did not play a leading part in that collection, to which we owe the place those letters fill in our New Testament. For Goodspeed's share in this argument see his *New Solutions of New Testament Problems,* where he points out (a) that before the publication of Acts, no Christian writer, not even the author of Acts himself, shows the least sign of acquaintance with any one of Paul's letters, or so much as a suspicion that Paul ever wrote a letter. (b) After the publication of Acts every Christian writing for the next fifty years or more shows itself profoundly influenced by Paul's letters as a collection. (c) In that collection Ephesians certainly had a part from the very first, and (d) its appearance in that collection is certainly its first appearance. For being, as all agree, an encyclical meant by its author to be read not by any single church only, but by all, or at least a circular to be read by a large group of churches, it must have received from the first, unlike the others, a considerable measure of publicity. If this happened in Paul's lifetime, its total disappearance by the time Acts was written, and 'Luke's' complete ignorance of it, no less than of the others, is 'an

53

insoluble riddle'. And who else but the maker of that collection can have written it? And where and when can he have done so, if not at Ephesus *c.* A.D. 90? And for what purpose, if not to serve as an introduction to the others and a help to their understanding?

V

But now the question arises, What became of that third letter (Col. iv. 16), which Tychicus and Onesimus took with them as far as Laodicea on the way to Colossae? Here we part company with Knox and Goodspeed. According to them it was none other than the letter we know as Philemon, and this was to be read in both churches in order to bring the pressure of Christian public opinion in both places to bear on the master of Onesimus, reinforcing Paul's appeal, and so make sure that he would set the youth free and return him to the Apostle.

But why should we imagine that Paul's friend cared what people might say in Laodicea and Colossae more than he cared how intensely Paul desired the liberation and return to himself of Onesimus, which was – as Knox has argued so convincingly – the main point of that letter? Why should we assume that Paul was so much less sure of his friend's consent than he professed to be in vs. 21? What becomes of his determination that whatever that friend does about this shall be of his own free will (vs. 14)? No, Lightfoot's comment, when Wieseler made long ago the same suggestion, still seems to hit the nail on the head – 'The theme, the treatment, the whole tenor of the letter, mark it as private. . . . The tact and delicacy of the Apostle's pleading for Onesimus would be nullified at one stroke by the demand for publication' (Lft., *Col. and Phmn.*, 1892, p. 279). Paul knew his friend far better than we do, and he had no doubt whatever that Philemon would seize this opportunity to refresh the heart of one to whom he owed so much.

Lightfoot's own view was that the letter referred to was Ephesians, which of course it could not be unless Paul wrote it. Many of us now agree that it was neither Philemon nor Ephesians nor any other of the Epistles now in existence under another name as listed by Lightfoot (Op. cit. p. 272). Only one possibility remains. As Moffatt pointed out long ago, 'No trace of this espistle is to be found, and it must be regarded as having perished at an early date after its composition' (*I.L.N.T.*, 1911, p. 160. So too S. Davidson, *Intr. to the study of the N.T.*, London, 1882, Vol. II, p. 194; Bernard Weiss, *A Manual of Introduction to the N.T.*, Berlin 1886, E. Transl. London, 1896, pp. 204, 333; C. H. Dodd, A.B.C., 1929, p. 1262). How this can have happened, we can only guess. My guess, as suggested in *Onesimus and Philemon*, is that its loss may have been due not to any carelessness on the part of some lukewarm custodian at Laodicea, but to an 'Act of God', such as one of those earthquakes from which Laodicea is known to have suffered as much as any city in that region. As Strabo says (578=xii, 16), εἰ γάρ τις ἄλλη, καὶ ἡ Λαοδίκεια εὔσειστος. We know from Tacitus, Ann. xiv. 27 that the city was laid low in the great earthquake of A.D. 60. If, as we have seen reason to believe, these three letters were sent *c.* A.D. 56, can any simpler or more natural explanation be imagined for the loss of this one some four years later?

If so, Onesimus must have known perfectly well that it would be no use trying to recover that letter thirty years later. There was only one thing to be done about that – and he, if anyone, was the man to do it – write another to take its place and represent it in the new collection. As part of the fiction that deceived nobody, and was not meant to deceive anyone, he would naturally call it 'to the Laodiceans', and this would be its original title, under which it appeared, as we know, in Marcion's Apostolicon. So Marcion was right about this, though he and Tertullian were both of them mistaken in thinking Paul had written it.

The shorter reading in i. 1 of our three most important MSS, B, ℵ, and now P⁴⁶ (this last *c.* A.D. 200) – τοῖς ἁγίοις τοῖς οὖσιν καὶ πιστοῖς – cannot be the original one, for, as E. Percy and C. Masson agree, it does not make any acceptable sense, but is obviously mutilated, and cries aloud for some place-name to fill the gap caused by the omission of the one its author gave it. This omission may well have been due to the waning reputation of Laodicea reflected in Rev. iii. 14-19.

This, and the very fact that Marcion favoured it, would settle the matter for many besides Tertullian, who failed to see that Marcion had no conceivable motive for making such a change, and that he had access to earlier evidence than they had. Then the claims of Ephesus, the mother-church and -city, proved irresistible for centuries, but surely not for ever, in favour of the one city of all others to which it is now unthinkable that either Paul or Onesimus writing in Ephesus itself under Paul's name, could have addressed it.

It will be seen that the Onesimus hypothesis now submitted makes no claim to originality – except perhaps in some details, and in the piecing together of many well-known facts, with others not so well-known, into a coherent whole. On the contrary, our indebtedness to other workers in this field will be apparent on every page. Of at least six famous scholars it must be said that each of them is the author of certain pages from which some essential feature of the present hypothesis was taken. It is here maintained that (1) Knox and (2) Goodspeed are right in believing the author of Ephesians to be Onesimus of Colossae, who c. A.D. 90 played a leading part in the collection of Paul's letters at Ephesus, and later, as bishop of Ephesus, visited Ignatius at Smyrna; (3) Duncan is right in his contention that Paul's letters to Philemon and the church at Colossae were written at Ephesus during a brief period of house-arrest (*libera custodia*) c. A.D. 56; (4) Moffatt was right in stressing and illustrating the contrast between the style of Ephesians and that of Paul, and in pointing out that no trace can be found of the letter which Paul sent to Laodicea at the same time as Colossians-Philemon, and it must have perished not long after its composition; (5) Holtzmann was right in maintaining that the author of Ephesians not only borrowed largely from Paul's original letter to the church at Colossae, but also added to that letter interpolations of his own, our Colossians being the result. (6) Our main authority for lexical data, such as the earliest known use of rare words, is Walter Bauer's Wörterbuch zum Neuen Testament (ed. 5, 1958), supported by the new Liddell and Scott (1940).

It has been suggested to me by Dr. G. B. Caird, as an objection to the hypothesis now submitted, that two passages here assigned to Onesimus, Eph. iv. 7-11 and Col. i. 15-18, have been shown by experts in Hebrew to be instances of St. Paul's knowledge of that language and of his acquaintance with Rabbinic Exegesis, whereas there is no evidence that Onesimus or any Gentile Christian knew Hebrew.

(1)

In *The Expositor* 1890 S. R. Driver pointed out that in Eph. iv. 8 ff., Διὸ λέγει, 'ANABÀC 'EIC ''YΨOC 'HXMAΛ-Ω'TEYCEN 'AIXMACΛΩI'AN, [KA'I'] ''EΔΩKEN ΔOM-ATA TO'IC 'ANΘP'ΩΠOIC, Psalm lxviii. 18 is quoted in a form which agrees neither with the Hebrew, "Thou hast ascended on high, thou hast led *thy* captivity captive, Thou hast received gifts among men," nor with the LXX, 'ANABAC 'EIC ''YΨOC 'HXMAΛΩ'TEYCAC 'AIXMA-ΛΩCI'AN ''EΛABEC ΔÓMATA 'EN 'ANΘP'ΩΠΩ (var. lect. 'EN 'ANΘPΩ'ΠOIC), but does agree with the Syriac Version and with the Targum, "Thou didst ascend to the firmament, Moses the prophet, thou didst take a captivity captive . . ., thou gavest gifts to the sons of men". Accordingly Driver regarded this as an instance of St. Paul's known acquaintance with, and use of, Rabbinic Exegesis.

Seven years later Abbott referred to these facts in his Commentary (p. 112 ff.), without mentioning Driver, and came to the same conclusion. "This Targum as we have it is of comparatively late date. But if we may assume, as no doubt we may, that it is giving us here an ancient interpretation, we have a solution of the difficulty, so far as St. Paul is concerned; he simply made use of the Rabbinic interpretation as being suitable to his purpose."

We may take it, then, as established that the author of Ephesians here shows his acquaintance with, and use of, Rabbinic Exegesis, and this is proof enough that he could read Hebrew. But while it is also quite certain that St. Paul knew Hebrew and was acquainted with Rabbinic interpretations of Scripture, it by no means follows that he was, as

Driver, Abbott and many others assume, the author of Ephesians. I can think of no reason why the fact, now established, that our author knew Hebrew and had some acquaintance with Rabbinic Exegesis, should make it any more difficult than before to believe that he was Onesimus once of Colossae, later of Ephesus. Though it might never have occurred to us, now that it is brought to our notice we can at least recognize in it the sort of idea that would appeal strongly to the devoted disciple, who cherished the memory of his great friend, and whole-heartedly believed Paul's Gospel. Would it not help him in his efforts to perpetuate that memory and to win fresh adherents for that Gospel, if he took steps to acquire a knowledge of that tongue and of those helps to the study of the scriptures which, as Onesimus knew even better than we do, had played so large a part in Paul's life and thought?

(2)

In an article on *Christ as the APXH of Creation* (J.T.S. XXVII, 1925-6, pp. 160 ff.) C. F. Burney showed Col. i. 15-18 to be 'an elaborate exposition of Bĕrêshîth in Genesis i, in the Rabbinic manner . . . Prov. viii. 12 ff., where Wisdom (i.e. Christ) is called rêshîth, gives the key to Gen. i. 1 "Berêshîth God created the heavens and the earth." In *Bĕrêshîth Rabba*, the great Midrashic commentary on Genesis, Rabbi Hosaiah (*c.* iii, A.D.) opens with a discussion of Prov. viii. 30. where Wisdom states "Then I was with him as a master workman ('āmôn)".'

This interpretation is supported by, among others, R. D. Davies in his great work *Paul and Rabbinic Judaism* (London, 1948, 1953, 1958, pp. 150 ff., 181). After reading what he and Burney have to say, I for my part regard it as established beyond reasonable doubt that whoever wrote this passage, Col. i. 15-18, must have known Hebrew and have been acquainted with Rabbinic interpretations of the Jewish Scriptures. Believing as I do that Onesimus was the author not only of Ephesians but also of the interpolated verses in Colossians, including i. 15-18, I find no difficulty whatever in accepting this as another example of his familiarity with

Rabbinic Expositions of Scripture current in his day.

Like Driver and Abbott, Burney and Davies hold the traditional opinion that St. Paul was the author of both Ephesians and the whole of Colossians, though scholars of their calibre are of course well aware that this particular tradition has long ceased to command universal consent. Davies recognizes that Col. i. 15-18 is 'one of the most disputed Christological passages in all the Pauline Epistles.' He knows all about F. C. Baur and the Tübingen School, about H. J. Holtzmann and his theories. He knows that more recently F. C. Porter 'has passionately rejected verses i. 15-17 as being incompatible with Paul's thought as a whole and irrelevant to the context in which they occur . . .' (*The Mind of Christ in Paul*, New York, 1930, p. 179 f.). But Davies is evidently unaware of the objective reasons given in this chapter and more fully in Chapter VII, for doubting the Pauline authorship of these and some other verses in Colossians as we have it. I venture to think that when he sees this evidence, he will not apply to it his own dictum, 'to solve our difficulties by recourse to the knife is to violate the objectivity which should characterize our study'. He and I are both of us convinced that the author of Ephesians was also the author of Col. i. 15 ff. He thinks Paul wrote them both, I think it was Onesimus. He may or may not find my reasons convincing, but they are as objective as his own.

When I wrote of Onesimus (p. 35 above), 'Here and there it seems to me that he knew how to put into words, and so make explicit, thoughts which are implicit in Paul's other letters, but nowhere else so explicit as here,' it was precisely such thoughts as the cosmological significance of Christ that I had in mind. That whoever wrote these verses was led to do this by the need to combat the Colossian heresy of his day, I hold as strongly as Davies does. But in my view, as explained in Chapter VII, the time when that heresy menaced the faith and loyalty of Christians in that area was more than a quarter-century after Paul's death. On this point I find the first paragraph in Chapter 8 of Davies's book (p. 177) most illuminating. "Important as it was . . . to assert the cosmic functions of Christ . . . it was chiefly the exigences of controversy that actually induced Paul to do so. Had it not been for the heresy at Colossae it is possible that we should never have had from the Apostle a fully articulated theory of Christ's agency in creation. Paul's interests lay elsewhere. Polemics might lead him to speculation on creation, but he was primarily concerned with redemption: more a missionary or an evangelist . . . than an apologetic theologian, it was with the moral and spiritual significance of Jesus that he would naturally be preoccupied."

So on Davies's own showing no such 'fully articulated theory of Christ's agency in creation' is to be found anywhere else in Paul's Epistles.

So too in that other passage interpolated, as I hold, by Onesimus, Col. ii. 6 b ff., describing the heresy that called forth this 'great Christology' of i. 15 ff., we meet for the first time in any 'Pauline' epistle those 'thrones' and 'dominations', in addition to the 'principalities and powers' of Rom. viii. 38 and 1 Cor. xv. 24, making a still wider range of the angelic hierarchies – 'world-rulers of this darkness', as they are called in Eph. vi. 12 – whose dwelling is in 'the heavenly places' presided over by 'the prince of the power of the air' – and all the superstitious beliefs and practices that go with them.

That Paul's mind was normally preoccupied with metaphysical speculations of this kind, Davies himself evidently does not believe any more than I do. As he says, "Paul's interests lay elsewhere". I could not agree more. That is exactly what I have been trying to say.

Taking (1) and (2) together, I cannot see that they weaken in any way the case for regarding Onesimus as the author of Ephesians and interpolator of Colossians. I can easily believe, on the strength of these two passages, that Onesimus had thought it worth his while to acquire a sufficient knowledge of Hebrew and acquaintance with the Rabbinic interpretations of Scripture current in his day – hoping thereby to improve his understanding of the Scriptures and his ability to interpret Paul.

(3)

If any doubt remained that the author of Ephesians could read Hebrew, it would be removed by the evidence that has recently come to hand in an article by K. G. Kuhn of Göttingen on *Der Epheserbrief im Lichte der Qumrantexte*, which was read to the S.N.T.S. at Aarhus in August 1960, and appears in New Testament Studies, Cambridge, July 1961.

Dr. Kuhn explicitly leaves out of account (1) Colossians and its relation to Ephesians, (2) the Pauline or non-Pauline authorship of Ephesians, and (3) the problem of its address, and confines himself to the question, to what extent and in what sense Ephesians shows a special relationship in language and in thought to the Qumran texts – whether a literary connexion is probable between Ephesians and the peculiar form of late Palestinian Judaism shown by the Qumran texts, (and by other forms of late Palestinian Judaism, especially the Jubilees, the Testaments of the XII Patriarchs, and the Enoch literature, all of which, it is highly probable, arose in the same Essene community).

In the first place, as pointed out by Klaus Beyer in a Dissertation at Heidelberg in 1960, the language and style of Ephesians is a Greek marked by Semitisms to a degree far in excess of all other Paulines. After a long list, almost identical with my own, of characteristic features distinguishing the style of Ephesians, Kuhn continues, 'All these peculiarities ... are also characteristic of the Hebrew style of the Qumran texts,' and concludes, 'So ist die Schlussfolgerung eines *Traditionszusammenhanges* des Epheserbriefes mit den Qumrantexten in Sprache und Stil kaum zu umgehen' (p. 337).

In the second place, Kuhn turns to the origin of the hortatory (paränetischen) tradition in the second main section of Ephesians (iv. 1-vi. 20). He produces instances which in his opinion show that a part of these exhortations is derived especially from the tradition of Essene exhortation (Paränese) as it lies before us in the Qumran texts and in late Jewish works akin to them.

The one and only hortatory section that does not show even a trace of relationship with the Qumran texts is the table of

61

duties to one's household (Haustafel) Eph. v. 22-vi. 9. Here we stand within *Hellenistic*-Jewish tradition, which goes back ultimately to the Stoa. In the Qumran texts there are no echoes of the syzygy of Christ and Church. There are indeed no parallels of any kind in Qumran to the Christology which in Ephesians included Ecclesiology. That was, of course, not to be expected in such a Jewish community as this (p. 346).

So far as I can see, the evidence now forthcoming leaves no room for doubt that whoever wrote Ephesians must have known enough Hebrew to enable him to study this late Jewish literature, that it must somehow and somewhere have been at his disposal, and that it had a profound effect on his style and on *some* of his ideas. This is entirely in keeping with the conclusion to which we were led by our inquiries in (1) and (2), that Onesimus may well have found it worth his while to add a knowledge of Hebrew to his other accomplishments. On the other hand this new evidence confronts those who still believe in the Pauline authorship of Ephesians with one more difficulty. For Paul's knowledge of Hebrew was not an accomplishment deliberately acquired by him as an adult, but a possession he had grown up with. This and his Rabbinic studies had quite a different effect both on his mind and on the style in which his letters were written.

VII

It only remains to offer a few remarks on the difference it would make to our reading of Ephesians, and our appreciation of its value, if the hypothesis now submitted were to meet with acceptance.

To people who have always read this Epistle as a crowning example of immortal literature produced by the Apostle Paul himself, it may be rather a shock when they are invited to believe that it was written by one who, so far from being an Apostle, makes his first appearance on the page of sacred history as a worthless slave (ἄχρηστος) who could not be trusted to do what he was told, unless someone stood by to see him do it, ('eye-service', ὀφθαλμοδουλία, as Paul called it, Col. iii. 22, and as he makes Paul call it again, Eph. vi. 6). But they may find it easier to accept this particular piece of modern criticism when they realize that one result of the change is to bring to light a great miracle of grace, that really did happen before the first Christian century was out. Obscured by a well-meant but erroneous tradition, and so forgotten through many centuries, it now appears that one of the most precious fruits of Paul's Gospel, as Paul himself preached it, was this young runaway slave, who had taken his master's money and spent it, and being at his wit's end, was persuaded by a good friend from Colossae, named Epaphras, to seek Paul's aid.

Thanks to two American scholars, John Knox and Edgar J. Goodspeed, it has been for some years clear to some of us, but ought to be more widely known, how Onesimus received from his new-found friend-in-need far more than he asked, or had dreamed anyone would ever give him, sympathy and understanding such as he did not know existed in this world, a promise of practical help; and with all this he heard Paul's own Good News Story told as only he could tell it. Never so long as he lived would Onesimus forget what he heard then. Yet even so, the giving was not all on one side. Paul's own life was enriched in that hour by the acquisition of a friend and helper well worth having ($\epsilon\check{v}\chi\rho\eta\sigma\tau\sigma s$), and more than that, a son, whom he had begotten in his bonds, a son in Christ. Not for the first time in his life, surely, the veteran preacher was moved to give his own soul along with the Gospel to an audience of one.

But this was only the beginning. We know too how Paul kept his promise of help by writing the letter that won for Onesimus the freedom he had longed for so passionately but hitherto in vain. Thanks to those same two scholars, we have learned to realize how right Paul was when he saw at once that there was far more in this youth than anyone else had imagined. For now we can see what good reasons there are for believing that it was this same Onesimus who thirty four years later played a leading part in collecting at Ephesus those letters which had lain for so long each in the strong-box of the church to which Paul had sent it, their very existence unsuspected by Christendom at large. By so doing he rescued them from present oblivion and possible destruction, and secured for them the place they have held ever since in the Christian Scriptures. In them as a collection Paul and the Gospel he preached still live on.

Nor is even this all that we owe to Onesimus. If he could not reproduce word for word the long-lost letter which he had himself accompanied to Laodicea, and had perhaps heard read aloud in Colossae, he could and did give us a better rendering than anyone else has ever done of the main elements in Paul's teaching as a whole and, by setting this at the forefront of Paul's own letters, make of them all, as Goodspeed has well said, 'one great encyclical' addressed to all Christians everywhere till the end of time.

That his own contemporaries did not fail to appreciate the magnitude of the services Onesimus had rendered, is proved by the fact that some years later we find him installed as bishop of Ephesus, in which capacity Ignatius on his way to martyrdom had reason to mention gratefully his 'well-loved name', and urged the Ephesians to show themselves worthy of the bishop God had given them, by a greater display of loyal obedience to him and of unity among themselves.

As more and more Christians come to realize how much we all owe to Onesimus, may not this knowledge itself help to bring nearer the day when that unity for which he pleaded so eloquently, and did so much, shall become an accomplished fact?

Meanwhile we may wonder what Paul himself would have said, if an angel from heaven had told him how that runaway slave from Colossae would someday requite what was done for him in that room at Ephesus where he entered the service that is perfect freedom.

CHAPTER VII
THE PROBLEM OF COLOSSIANS

For quite a long time now nearly all British New Testament scholars have been agreed that St. Paul wrote Colossians, the only question being when and where he did so. This question has been a live one since 1929, when G. S. Duncan's book, St. Paul's Ephesian Ministry, made known the results of Deissmann's suggestion to its author five years earlier that he should look into the hypothesis that St. Paul's four 'prison letters' were written not from Rome but from Ephesus. 'It was not long,' Duncan told us, before he 'became convinced that the Imprisonment Epistles are all to be assigned to the three years which the apostle spent in Asia'.

Notwithstanding the silence of Acts about any such imprisonment, a considerable body of experts can now be quoted in favour of the opinion that Paul wrote some of his prison letters at Ephesus. But there is nothing like the same agreement as to which of them were written there. Some say Philippians but not Colossians and Philemon, others say Colossians and Philemon but not Philippians. Meanwhile the number of those who think Paul wrote Ephesians at Ephesus or anywhere else keeps on dwindling.

There remains the hard core of resistance, with C. H. Dodd for its spokesman, who will have none of this Ephesian theory in any of its forms, and maintains that 'the case for placing Philippians during an imprisonment at Ephesus breaks down,' . . . and 'the case for an Ephesian origin of Colossians does not so much break down as go by default. There is no case to send to the jury.' (New Testament Studies, Manchester, 1954, p. 103f.). To this and other criticisms Duncan replied in The Expository Times and in New Testament Studies (Cambridge), showing himself quite unmoved, except in very minor details, from his original position.

Between these mutually contradictory views the present

position looks like a deadlock, and it seems pertinent to suggest a third alternative. May not each of these two protagonists have grasped a truth which has eluded the other? And can both be mistaken about the one point on which they are agreed – the mistake being due in both cases to their having overlooked certain essential facts? As Dodd says, 'The best hypothesis is that which accounts for the largest number of relevant facts' (op. cit. p. 107).

One such fact, which no one who attempts to solve the problem of Colossians can afford to leave out of account, but which seems to have escaped the notice of many scholars, including the two just named, is the extraordinary number of New Testament *Hapax Legomena*, and other words not to be found elsewhere in the Paulines, that are massed together in a single passage, Col. ii. 8-23. Here in just over a page we find no fewer than sixteen of the thirty three "Hapax Leg." listed under Colossians in Appendix I C1, p. 146 of *P.P.E.*

They are συλαγωγέω, φιλοσοφία, θεότης, σωματικῶς, ἀπέκδυσις, χειρόγραφον, προσηλόω, ἀπεκδύομαι, νεομηνία, καταβραβεύω, ἐμβατεύω, δογματίζομαι, ἀπόχρησις, ἐθελοθρησκεία, ἀφειδία and πλησμονή.

In the Pastoral Epistles, which neither Dodd nor Duncan believes to have been written by St. Paul, "Hapax Leg." average 12·8 per page, in 2 Tim. 12·9, in Tit. 16·1 and in 1 Tim. 15·2, as we have seen *P.P.E.* p. 21, Diagram I.

Of twenty two words found elsewhere in the New Testament, but in no other Pauline (Appendix I C2), nine are in this same passage – ἐξαλείφω, ὑπεναντίον, δειγματίζω, σκία, ἑορτή, θρησκεία, γεύω, θιγγάνω and ἔνταλμα.

With C1 these make twenty five C words, as compared with 22·3 such words per page in the Pastorals (A1 and 2), 24·2 in 2 Tim., 27 in 1 Tim. and 30·1 in Tit. (*P.P.E.* p. 25, Diagram II).

As with the Pastoral "Hapax Leg.", so here, most of these occur also in writers before or during Paul's lifetime, as well as long after it. But here too we find several which, so far as I can discover, do not occur otherwise till the turn of the century or later still – συλαγωγέω, θεότης, ἀπέκδυσις, νεομηνία (before ii A.D. always in the contracted form νουμηνία), ἐθελοθρησκεία.

Shared exclusively with Ephesians we find συζωοποιέω, ἁφή and αὔξησις: also συνεγείρω only here and iii. 1, Eph. ii. 6.

Nor is it only in vocabulary that this passage shows a marked contrast with the genuine Paulines. Its style has the same chracteristics which have convinced so many experts that Ephesians is the work of another than Paul – the long, laboured sentence with one subordinate clause after another, full of participles and relative pronouns, eight verses covering nearly half a page before we come to a full stop; the genitival formations, the most unpauline superabundance of synonymns, the strange employment of the preposition ἐν far in excess of the normal Pauline average, 116 (plus four?) in the eight and three quarter pages of Ephesians, or 13·25 per page, (Rom. 6·7, 1 Cor. 7·1, 2 Cor. 9·7, Gal. 5, Phil. 10·5, 1 Thess. 9, 2 Thess 9, Phmn. 7·2, Col. ii. 8-23 16 (in thirty three and a half lines).[1]

On the other hand, of the Pauline Particles, Prepositions &c. listed on p. 36 f. of *P.P.E.* Romans has (including repetitions) 187 or 7·2 per page, 1 Cor. 12 per page, 2 Cor. 9·9, Gal. 10·8, Eph. 4·3, Phil. 9, 1 Thess. 9·3, 2 Thess. 5, Phmn. 12·8. Col. ii. 8-23 has only ὑπενάντιος, εἰκῇ and σύν (bis), and one of these, ὑπενάντιος, occurs in the New Testament only here and Heb. x. 27, so is Pauline only if Paul wrote this passage. So Ephesians has fewer than any Pauline, and this passage has fewer still. I can no more believe Paul wrote this passage than I can believe he wrote the Pastorals.

But I can and do believe it was written by the author of Ephesians, who is identified by Goodspeed and Knox, I think rightly, with Onesimus of Colossae, who under Heaven owed everything to Paul – his conversion, his freedom from salvery, his growing influence in the churches of the Lycus valley and in Ephesus after Paul's martyrdom, his eventual appointment as bishop of Ephesus, the metropolis of that

---

[1]The recurrence of ἐν in 2 Cor. vi. 4-7, nineteen times in seven lines, and 2 Cor. xi. 23-27, thirteen times in ten lines, is of course quite a different thing, and would never cause anyone to question the Pauline authorship of these verses.

region – and who, we believe, took a leading part in that collection of Paul's letters *c.* A.D. 90, which was to form the nucleus of our New Testament. This is indeed, as Goodspeed calls it, 'a conjecture,' but it is one that conflicts with no fact known to me, and is the only hypothesis which accounts convincingly, to my mind, for all the relevant facts, including some (like the inclusion of Philemon in that collection, and the unparalleled use of Colossians-Philemon by the author of Ephesians), which would otherwise seem inexplicable.

Another mark of his style which has struck many scholars, is his use of 'redundant epexegetic formations' (Moffatt), his 'coupling of two synonymous nouns by means of a genitive' (Jülicher), like βουλὴ τοῦ θελήματος (Eph. i. 11), κράτος τῆς ἰσχύος (Eph. i. 19, vi. 10, Col. i. 11), μεσοτοίχιον τ. φραγμοῦ (Eph. ii. 14) &c. (Mitton, p. 11). So here τοῦ σώματος τῆς σαρκός (Col. i. 22, ii. 11).

Here too are those familiar phrases borrowed from Paul's own epistles, of which we find such an abundance in Ephesians – κατὰ τὴν παράδοσιν 2 Thess. iii. 6 (cf. Mk. vii. 5 κατὰ τὴν παράδοσιν τῶν πρεσβυτέρων), τὰ στοιχεῖα τοῦ κόσμου, and again τῶν στοιχείων τοῦ κόσμου = Gal. iv. 3, πάσης ἀρχῆς καὶ ἐξουσίας, and again τὰς ἀρχὰς καὶ τὰς ἐξουσίας, echoing 1 Cor. xv. 24, as in Eph. i. 21, συνταφέντες αὐτῷ ἐν τῷ βαπτίσματι recalling Rom. vi. 4, Θεοῦ τοῦ ἐγείραντος αὐτὸν ἐκ νεκρῶν from Gal. i. 1, ἐν βρώσει καὶ ἐν πόσει Rom. xiv, 17, (σκία τῶν μελλόντων Heb. x. 1), τὸ σῶμα τοῦ Χριστοῦ Rom. vii. 4, 1 Cor. x. 16, xii. 27, εἰ ἀπεθάνετε σὺν Χριστῷ Rom. vi. 8, ἐν κόσμῳ Rom. v. 13, 1 Cor. viii. 4 &c.

But, it may be objected, if those *Hapax Legomena* prove that Paul did not write this passage, do they not equally prove that it cannot have been written by the author of Ephesians, since they are as foreign to that epistle as they are to the other Paulines? The answer to that is No. For Ephesians, though it tells us quite a lot about its author, if we read it rightly, is much too small a specimen of his handiwork to justify the kind of inference we may reasonably draw from the many times greater bulk of genuine Pauline matter before us. It is not even as if Ephesians were, like each of the other Paulines, intended by its author to convey to its readers an expression in his own words of his own views and wishes. Ephesians was evidently meant to be, as it is in fact, a summary of the Apostle's teaching as a whole, couched for the most part in the Apostle's own words. After setting aside its borrowings from the other Paulines, all that is left of it fills no more than a fraction of its eight and three quarter pages. It would be fantastic to use so diminutive a selection from this man's vocabulary as evidence that he could not have written the paragraph now in question, which in other respects shows all the distinctive marks of his style.

Yet one more piece of evidence, clinching the rest, and showing who must be the author of this passage, since it cannot be Paul, is the series of phrases strongly reminiscent of Ephesians – περιτομῇ ἀχειροποιήτῳ . . . τῇ ἀκροβυστίᾳ τῆς σαρκός . . . (Eph. ii. 11 οἱ λεγόμενοι ἀκροβυστία ὑπὸ τῆς λεγομένης περιτομῆς ἐν σαρκὶ χειροποιήτου), πᾶν τὸ πλήρωμα τῆς θεότητος (Eph. iii. 19 πᾶν τὸ πλήρωμα τοῦ θεοῦ), καὶ ὑμᾶς νεκροὺς ὄντας τοῖς παραπτώμασιν ὑμῶν συνεζωοποίησεν σὺν αὐτῷ (Eph. ii. 1 καὶ ὑμᾶς ὄντας νεκροὺς τοῖς παραπτώμασιν ὑμῶν, Eph. ii. 5 καὶ ὄντας ἡμᾶς νεκροὺς τοῖς παραπτώμασιν συνεζωοποίησεν τῷ Χριστῷ),τὴν κεφαλήν, ἐξ οὗ πᾶν τὸ σῶμα διὰ τῶν ἁφῶν καὶ συνδέσμων ἐπιχορηγούμενον καὶ συμβιβαζόμενον αὔξει τήν αὔξησιν . . . (Eph. iv. 15 f., ἡ κεφαλή, . . . ἐξ οὗ πᾶν τὸ σῶμα συναρμολογούμενον καὶ συμβιβαζόμενον διὰ πάσης ἁφῆς τῆς ἐπιχορηγίας . . . τὴν αὔξησιν τοῦ σώματος ποιεῖται . . .).

But is this the only passage in which this inspired interpreter of St. Paul has added to Paul's original letter something that he believed would convey to its readers the mind of his revered teacher in its relevance to the needs and problems of their own day? There is certainly no other such array of *Hapax Legomena*. But it was not its *Hapax Legomena* that led us to ascribe Col. ii. 8-23 to the author of Ephesians. What they did was to convince us that it was not St. Paul. And there is another passage of about the same length, i. 9b-25 (ἐν πάσῃ σοφίᾳ . . . λόγον τοῦ θεοῦ), which shows all those other characteristics that we have learnt to recognize as distinctive features of the style in which Ephesians is written.

In the first place we find here the longest of all those long, laboured sentences, with one participial or relative clause after another, covering more than a page of thirty three lines before we come to a full stop.

Here, as in ii. 8-23, we find the same genitival coupling of the same two synonymous nouns, ἐν τῷ σώματι τῆς σαρκός. Other genitival formations are κράτος τῆς δόξης, (κράτος only here and Eph. i. 19, vi. 10 and other New Testament books, but not in Paul), μερίδα τοῦ κλήρου, (ἐξουσία τοῦ σκότους =Lk. xxii. 53), υἱοῦ τῆς ἀγάπης, αἵματος τοῦ σταυροῦ, τῆς ἐλπίδος τοῦ εὐαγγελίου.

Also the preposition ἐν used fourteen times, and the same paucity of those Pauline Particles, Prepositions &c. listed on p. 36 f. of *P.P.E.* – κατενώπιον, νυνὶ δέ, γε and εἴτε . . . εἴτε. Of these the first occurs only here, in Eph. i, 4 and Ju. 24.

On this page there is no question-mark, on ii. 8-23 only one, as in Ephesians.

Here too are the same frequent borrowings from one Pauline after another – εἰς πᾶσαν ὑπομονήν (2 Cor. xii. 2 ἐν πάσῃ ὑπομονῇ), μετὰ χαρᾶς (=Phil. i. 3, 1 Thess. i. 6), ὃς ἐρύσατο ἡμᾶς ἐκ . . . (2 Cor. i. 10), ἐν τοῖς ἔθνεσιν Rom. i. 5, 13, 1 Cor. v. 1, Gal. i. 16, ii. 2), ὅς ἐστιν εἰκὼν τοῦ θεοῦ 2 Cor. iv. 4, ἐν τοῖς οὐρανοῖς 2 Cor. v. 1, εἴτε τὰ ἐπὶ τῆς γῆς εἴτε τὰ ἐν τοῖς οὐρανοῖς (1 Cor. viii. 5 εἴτε ἐν οὐρανῷ εἴτε ἐπὶ γῆς, Eph. i. 10 τὰ ἐπὶ τοῖς οὐρανοῖς καὶ τὰ ἐπὶ τῆς γῆς), ἄρχαι . . . ἐξουσίαι 1 Cor. xv. 24, Col. ii. 10, Eph. i. 21, iii. 10, vi. 12), τὰ πάντα δι' αὐτοῦ καὶ εἰς αὐτόν Rom. xi. 36, νυνὶ δέ Rom. vi. 22 &c., ἀποκατήλλαξεν διὰ τοῦ θανάτου (Rom. v. 10 εἰ . . . κατηλλάγημεν τῷ θεῷ διὰ τοῦ θανάτου . . .), εἴ γε (Rom. v. 6, 2 Cor. v. 3, Gal. iii. 4). εἰ ἐπιμένετε (Rom. xi, 22 ἐὰν ἐπιμένῃς), ἑδραῖοι καὶ μὴ μετακινούμενοι (1 Cor. xv. 58 ἑδραῖοι . . . ἀμετακίνητοι), τοῦ εὐαγγελίου . . . τοῦ κηρυχθέντος . . . (Gal. ii. 2 τὸ εὐαγγέλιον ὃ κηρύσσω), νῦν χαίρω = 2 Cor. vii. 9, ἐν τῇ σαρκί μου =Rom. vii. 18, Gal. iv. 14, (cf. Eph. ii.4 ἐν τῇ σαρκὶ αὐτοῦ), ἐγὼ Παῦλος =2 Cor. x. 1, Gal. v. 2, 1 Thess. ii. 18, Phmn. 19, τὸν λόγον τοῦ θεοῦ=Phil. i. 14.

Like ii. 8-23 this passage has unmistakable correspondences of word and phrase with Ephesians, often assumed to be cases of borrowing from this Pauline epistle by the author of Ephesians, but equally consistent, (as Conservative scholars maintain) with identity of authorship, only as I suggest, the author of both is here Onesimus. Shared exclusively with

70

Ephesians are ἀποκαταλλάσσω (bis) and Eph. ii. 16, and κυριότητες plural = 'dominions' (in the angelic hierarchy, Eph. i. 21. In Jude and 2 Peter singular, with quite a different meaning); shared with Ephesians and other New Testament books but no Pauline, κράτος Eph. i. 19, vi. 10, Luke-Acts &c., κατενώπιον Eph. i. 4, Jude. Also the phrases ἐν ᾧ ἔχομεν τὴν ἀπολύτρωσιν, τὴν ἄφεσιν τῶν ἁμαρτιῶν ... διὰ τοῦ αἵματος ... αὐτοῦ (Eph. i. 7 ἐν ᾧ ἔχομεν τὴν ἀπολύτρωσιν διὰ τοῦ αἵματος αὐτοῦ, τὴν ἄφεσιν τῶν παραπτωμάτων), τοῦ εὐαγγελίου ... οὗ ἐγενόμην ἐγὼ Παῦλος διάκονος (Eph. iii. 6 τοῦ εὐαγγελίου οὗ ἐγενήθην διάκονος, Eph. iii. 1 ἐγὼ Παῦλος), ἁγίους καὶ ἀμώμους κατενώπιον αὐτοῦ = Eph. i. 4, χαίρω ἐν τοῖς παθήμασιν ὑπὲρ ὑμῶν ... θλίψεσιν ... (Eph. iii. 13 ... ἐν τοῖς θλίψεσίν μου ὑπὲρ ὑμῶν), τοῦ σώματος αὐτοῦ, ὅ ἐστιν ἡ ἐκκλησία (Eph. i. 23 τῇ ἐκκλησίᾳ, ἥτις ἐστὶν τὸ σῶμα αὐτοῦ), τὴν οἰκονομίαν τοῦ θεοῦ τὴν δοθεῖσάν μοι εἰς ὑμᾶς (Eph. iii. 2 τὴν οἰκονομίαν τῆς χάριτος τοῦ θεοῦ τῆς δοθείσης μοι εἰς ὑμᾶς).

Here are five more *Hapax Legomena*, ἀνταναπληρόω, εἰρηνοποιέω, μετακινέω, ὁρατός and πρωτεύω, and the un-Pauline words δυναμόω (Heb. xi. 34) and θρόνοι (plus New Testament, but only here in plural = angelic hierarchies).

The writer's purpose in adding these two passages to the original letter was evidently to bring out the cosmic significance of Christ as Lord of the whole universe seen and unseen, through whom and for whom all things in heaven and earth were created, Head of the one Church which is His body, in Whom dwells all the fulness of the Godhead, Who by His death on the cross has won for all believers forgiveness and a share in the peace that follows His victory over all the powers of darkness, those angelic hierarchies – 'thrones, dominions, principalities and powers' – which, according to the philosophic theories current at the time of writing, constituted the links of a chain connecting the absolute and unapproachable Deity with this material world. By making this supremacy of Christ clear and explicit, as he was sure the Apostle would have done had he been still alive, he hoped to strengthen and confirm the faith of his fellow Christians in the regions he knew so well, and throughout the world, and to bring home to them the folly and futility of those errors

71

– a mixture of Jewish elements with oriental speculations –
which were leading many to accept a less exalted conception
of Christ, and adopt practices such as the worship of angels,
perverse types of asceticism, and the observation of special
rites at the time of the new moon.

All this was of course set forth long ago in masterly fashion
by Lightfoot, who, however, was himself misled by his mistaken belief that Paul wrote the Pastoral Epistles as well as
Ephesians, to date these developments during Paul's lifetime.
'The heresies of the Pastoral Epistles are the heresies of the
Colossians and Ephesians grown rank and corrupt' (Phil.,
1894, p. 45). Similarly Zahn „Am ersten noch scheinen die
sogenannten Irrlehrer der Pastoralbriefe Beruhrungspunkte
mit denjenigen des Kl zu zeigen; aber sie gehören der
Lebenszeit des Pl an" (Einl. N.T., 1906, I, p. 354).

Once it is recognized that the Pastorals were written under
Trajan and Hadrian, their evidence, like that of Ephesians
and these verses in Colossians, points rather to a date c.
A.D. 90 for the errors here combated, i.e. before Cerinthus
who, as Lightfoot showed, went further than anything suggested in these passages.

With these exceptions, we find very little else in this
Epistle that could not perfectly well have been dictated (or
written, iv. 18) by the Apostle himself.

The brief parenthesis 6b (καθὼς καὶ ἐν παντὶ . . . καθὼς καὶ
ἐν ὑμῖν), with its awkward duplication of καθὼς καί, its exag-
gerated claim that the Gospel has already been preached in
all the world, (as in vs. 23 'to every creature under heaven'),
and its curious anticipation of the words 'bearing fruit and
increasing' in vs. 10 as already taking place 'in all the world
even as in you also', looks more like the enthusiastic disciple
making a claim for the Apostle which Clement too makes for
him only a very few years later, (1 Clem. v. 7 δικαιοσύνην
διδάξας ὅλον τὸν κόσμον) than Paul speaking for himself.

In ii. 2b-4 (συμβιβασθέντες . . . πιθανολογίᾳ), the first word
='knit together' as in Eph. iv. 16 and Col. ii. 19 – contrast
1 Cor. ii, 16, where it means 'instruct' – and the last word is
yet another *Hapax Legomenon* while ἀπόκρυφος and παραλογίζο-
μαι are both foreign to the Paulines. The purpose of this

72

insertion is made clear in vs. 4. It is to render its readers immune from the grave danger of having their minds poisoned by the plausible words of some who are trying to lead them away from the true faith briefly expressed in verses 2 and 3. This is manifestly the same conception of the true faith as we have found insisted upon, and stated at greater length, in our two major interpolations, and the specious errors here denounced can be none other than those against which this same writer urges them to stand firm in i. 23, and describes more fully in ii. 16 ff. In the original letter vs. ii. 5 follows on from ii. 1, 2a (. . . αἱ καρδίαι αὐτῶν) much better without this interruption than with it.

Having come so far, I find it quite impossible to believe that ii. 7 can be part of the original letter. Having bidden the Colossians, as they had received Jesus Christ the Lord, to walk in Him, (an apt and favourite metaphor), the real Paul would not in the same breath continue, 'rooted and builded up in Him' – as if, like the blind man in Mark viii. 24, only more so, he could see men as trees *and houses* walking! But the author of Ephesians could, as we know, take such mixtures of metaphors in his stride – e.g. iii. 17 ἐρριζωμένοι καὶ τεθεμελιωμένοι . . . 'with deep roots and firm foundations, may you be strong to grasp . . .' (N.E.B.).

So ii. 7 heads our major interpolation ii. 8-23, the original letter breaks off at the end of ii, 6, and the next question is, where is it resumed? In itself iii. 1 could have been written by either Paul or Onesimus. But this verse (εἰ οὖν συνηγέρθητε . . . ΚΑΘΗ'ΜΕΝΟΣ) is clearly a continuation not of ii. 6 but of ii. 7-23. συνεγείρω occurs elsewhere only Col. ii, 12 and Eph. ii, 6, εἰ οὖν συνηγέρθητε corresponds to the εἰ ἀπεθάνετε σὺν . . . of ii. 20, whereas it makes no sense after the εἰ οὖν παρελάβετε . . . of ii. 6. τὰ ἄνω ζητεῖτε serves as a transition to τὰ ἄνω φρονεῖτε. 'ΕΝ ΔΕΞΙΑ . . . ΚΑΘΗ'ΜΕΝΟΣ, derived ultimately from Psalm cxi, can here be equally well assigned to the author of Eph. i. 20 (who had certainly read Rom. viii. 34), as to Paul.

From here to the end of Colossians the only lines that to my mind read like a possible insertion are iii. 14-16. I incline to agree here with Masson (Col. p. 144). For σύνδεσμος cf. ii. 19 and Eph. iv. 3 συνδέσμῳ τῆς εἰρήνης . For the rest cf. Eph. v. 19.

On the whole Epistle I feel, with all due respect, that Masson's fifteen interpolations are too many, and that the original Pauline letter was much longer than he allows. Still, Masson's solution of these two closely interrelated problems and my own, being fundamentally the same, though arrived at independently and by different paths, seem to me to help one another considerably. That we differ in some details, while we agree in many others, was only to be expected. Though I naturally prefer my own, I am much more sure that our solution is in the main true, than I am about some of these minor details. For instance, he may well be right in claiming for Paul the words συνταφέντες αὐτῷ ἐν τῷ βαπτίσματι (ii. 12, cf. Rom. vi. 4), on the ground that the author of Ephesians had not appropriated this doctrine. But that he is right in regarding ii. 8 f. (βλέπετε μή τις ὑμᾶς ἔσται ὁ *συλαγωγῶν διὰ τῆς *φιλοσοφίας κ.τ.λ.) as part of the original letter, I cannot believe.

However, I submit with some confidence that all the complex phenomena brought to light by a close study of the language of Colossians cannot be reconciled with the Pauline authorship of this Epistle as a whole. The only hypothesis that is consistent with all the relevant data is one that was framed for the sole purpose of accounting for them – i.e. that our Colossians is a genuine Pauline letter with interpolations by the author of Ephesians – as Holtzmann saw long ago, though he failed to produce a convincing account of the details.[1] The original letter can only be the one Paul wrote at Ephesus c. A.D. 56 and sent along with Philemon by the hand of Tychicus (iv. 7), who was accompanied by the Onesimus named in them both. But, as we have seen in Chapter VI, the author of Ephesians was that same Onesimus, who c. A.D. 90 collected Paul's letters at Ephesus, and included this one of his own, intending it to replace and represent in the new collection Paul's long lost letter to the Laodiceans (Col. iv. 16), and to serve as a summary of Paul's teaching and an

---

[1] For a list of earlier unsuccessful attempts to work out this interpolation theory in detail see Josef Schmid, Der Epheserbrief des Ap. Paulus, 1928, p. 394.

introduction to his letters as a whole – a purpose for which it is admirably fitted.

Only on this assumption does the unique relation between these two Epistles become clear. Each helps us to understand the other, and without that help neither is fully intelligible. The final proof that Ephesians is pseudonymous is found in Colossians. For the interpolations in Colossians are in the inimitable style of Ephesians, and as it happens at least one of those interpolations (ii. 7-iii. 1) taken as all of a piece can no more have been written by St. Paul than 1 Timothy can – the Pastoral Epistle in which no genuine note has been embodied by its author, though it does contain, like Ephesians and the interpolations in Colossians, a number of phrases manifestly borrowed from the genuine Pauline Epistles.

The genuine letter of Paul to the church at Colossae, as I see it, then, consisted of Col. i. 1-6a (Παῦλος . . . παρόντος εἰς ὑμᾶς), i. 6c-9a (ἀφ᾿ ἧς ἡμέρας . . . θελήματος αὐτοῦ), i. 26-2a (τὸ μυστήριον . . . καρδίαι αὐτῶν), ii, 5, 6 (εἰ γὰρ . . . περιπατεῖτε), iii. 2-13 (τὰ ἄνω φρονεῖτε . . . οὕτως καὶ ὑμεῖς), iii. 17-iv. 18 (καὶ πᾶν ὅ τι . . . μεθ᾿ ὑμῶν) – a little more than half of our Colossians.

It was written at Ephesus c. A.D. 56 during a brief period of house arrest by friendly Asiarchs (Acts xix. 31), to keep Paul out of the reach of fanatical Jews, and avert a riot, and it was sent along with Philemon and the letter to Laodicea which perished not many years later. These three letters were carried by Tychicus, who was accompanied by Onesimus himself. The one to the church at Colossae was written at the request of its founder Epaphras, himself a convert of the Apostle, who had preached the Gospel on Paul's behalf to his own folk in the city where he belonged (i. 7, iv. 12 ὁ ἐξ ὑμῶν).

We note first that the 'church' in this letter is still, as nearly always in Paul's other letters, the local community of saints, whether at Colossae or Laodicea, or the still smaller company meeting in the private house of Philemon at Colossae, or of Nympha at Laodicea. Next, there is not a word in it about any trouble due to heretical propaganda. It is not surprising to find that this little church had so far escaped that sort of disturbance. For it cannot have been in existence for more

75

than a year or two. Had that sort of disturbance already arisen among them, Paul would no doubt have expressed his amazement that they had so quickly let themselves be led astray (Gal. i. 6).

Such discord as there was between its members was due to quite different causes – the immaturity of these beginners in the Christian way of life, their failure to realize that racial antipathies (iii. 11), class distinctions (ibid.), intolerance and censoriousness (iii. 13) and the like have no place in a truly Christian society – and apparently the relapse of a few into still lower depths of heathenism (iii. 5-7), not to mention bad temper, bad language and insincerity in word or deed (iii. 8 f.).

But on the whole Epaphras had been able to report a much happier state of things in this very young church, and the keynote of Paul's charge to them is struck in his first word. He and Timothy thank God for their steadfast faith, and their love toward all the saints. Though absent from them in the flesh, he is in spirit watching with joy the 'order' prevailing in their ranks.

They are divided, but not against one another, by a wholly natural classification, into husbands and wives, parents and children, also (as things are now) masters and slaves. A brief word on the mutual duties of the first two pairs prepares for a fuller injunction to the third pair, which is actually the occasion and in a sense the main purpose of the letter – at least in the eyes of Onesimus – to support the one to Philemon.

In this form the letter surely 'authenticates itself', as Dodd says of Philemon. There is nothing either in its style and diction or in its subject-matter to conflict with the hypothesis that it and Philemon were written at Ephesus c. A.D. 56 during a brief period of house arrest.

In neither of these two letters do we find the slightest hint that Paul's life was in danger, or that before he could hope to pay that visit to Colossae he must first stand on trial before Caesar on a capital charge. This is surely a more serious objection to the traditional theory that Paul wrote them in Rome than its advocates seem to realize. This and the thirteen hundred miles journey from Rome to Colossae combine to make Paul's request for a lodging to be prepared forthwith (ἅμα δὲ πάι) to my mind irreconcilable with the Roman hypothesis.

As we have already seen in Chapter VI above, p. 43, the distance of all those journeys to and fro between Colossae and wherever Paul was when he wrote those two letters – journeys assumed to have been made quite recently or contemplated in the near future – adds up to a total of more than eight thousand miles, if Paul was in Rome, nine hundred if he was at Ephesus.

All things considered, I find the case for Duncan's theory, that Ephesus was the birthplace and c. A.D. 56 the date of Colossians-Philemon, much stronger than he made it.

Thirty four years later it may well have occurred to Onesimus that, if only Paul could have anticipated the kind of false teaching that was now troubling not only the church at Colossae but the whole Church in that area, he would surely have included in his letter some clear warning against such attempts to whittle down the glory of Christ, and some explicit statement of those high truths which are implicit in all his letters, and are the essence of his Gospel as Onesimus understood it. Then future readers of this wonderful letter might have been helped to see in its larger setting what Paul himself had meant, when he wrote about his great open secret, that mystery of mysteries, hid from so many ages and generations, now at long last revealed to the saints, 'God in Christ' and 'Christ in you, the hope of glory.'

If, with this in mind, Onesimus felt moved to add to this letter, which meant so much to him, what he sincerely believed the Apostle would have added had he known what the future had in store for Christ's people, who shall deny that what moved him was the same Spirit that had moved his great friend and teacher?

To a modern scholar, as he studies this Epistle in the cold light of reason, with all the critical apparatus at his disposal, these interpolations stand out like patches of new cloth on an old garment. But they were not written to baffle the scrutiny of twentieth century critics, but to strengthen the faith and deepen the devotion of Christian men and women hard pressed by the temptations of this world. And they have served that purpose through more generations than either Paul or Onesimus could foresee.

CHAPTER VIII

Romans i. 19–ii. 1

A SECOND-CENTURY INTERPOLATION

That Rom. i. 19-ii. 1 had no place in Marcion's Apostolicon
has been known since Zahn's reconstruction of the text in his
Geschichte des Neutestamentlichen Kanons (Erlangen-Leipzig,
1892, Vol. II, p. 516), and still more widely recognized as an
established fact since Harnack's *Marcion* (Leipzig, 1920,
1924², pp. 48, 103*). As evidence of this fact both Zahn and
Harnack give Tertullian, *Adv. Marc.* V 13 'Quoniam et iram
dicit revelari de coelo super impietatem et iniustitiam homi-
num' (=Rom. i. 18 omitting 'dei' after 'iram' and 'omnem'
before 'impietatem')[1] . . . Etiam adiiciens: Scimus autem
iudicium dei secundum veritatem esse' (=Rom. ii. 2a), showing that in Marcion's text i. 18 was followed immediately by
ii. 2a – „so war bei ihm II 2 unmittelbar mit I 18 verbunden."
Harnack held (against Zahn) that ii. 2b τοὺς τὰ τοιαῦτα
πράσσοντας was probably included in Marcion's text, „da es
sich gut zu I 18 fügt."

Harnack saw no reason to doubt that Marcion did in fact
cut out from the text before him a great many genuine passages, as stated by Tertullian and the rest of our sources. In
some cases the gaps ('foveas') made by these excisions came
to as much as a page, in others to several consecutive pages,
though for the most part they were much shorter than that.

But then came P. L. Couchoud with his theory that it was
Marcion who in his shorter version preserved the original
text of Paul's epistles, and that the longer version of our
manuscripts is marred by numerous interpolations and
falsifications, the work of catholic editors later than Marcion

---

[1] For Harnack's proof that Tertullian had Marcion's Apostolicon before
him in a slavishly litteral Latin translation, from which it is hardly ever
difficult to recover the Greek original, see his Marcion, pp. 48*–56*.

and a hundred years after St. Paul (*La première édition de Sain Paul, Revue de l'histoire des religions*, Paris, 1926).

Today most of us who have studied both are convinced that Harnack was right in his general conclusion, and Couchoud mistaken. It seems clear that Marcion himself, and his followers who carried his 'corrections' further still, regarded his work not as preserving the Pauline text before him but as restoring the original which he found already corrupted by 'pseudapostoli nostri et Judaici evangelizatores' (Tert. *Adv. Marc.* V 19, Harn. *M*, p. 46*. Cf. Tert. *Adv. Marc.* I 20, Harn. *M*, p. 42 'Aiunt enim Marcionem non tam innovasse regulam . . . quam retro adulteratam recurasse').

But, as we shall see presently, for reasons overlooked both by Harnack and by Couchoud, as well as by many other scholars, among all the numerous passages in our accepted text which did not appear in Marcion's Apostolicon, Rom. i. 19-ii. 1 is in a class by itself, and in this particular instance Harnack was in all probability mistaken, and Couchoud came nearer to the truth than he himself realized.

According to Harnack there is nothing exceptional here. These verses, like so many others, were very probably erased (getilgt) *M.* p. 103*). Marcion struck out θεοῦ after ὀργή in i. 18 „weil der gute Gott night zürnt,“ and rejected the whole of i. 19-ii. 1 because this piece of natural religion was bound to be just as repugnant to him as was the thought that men were given over to the blackest vices as a punishment (zur Strafe p. 48). There is indeed little room for doubt that Marcion would never have allowed this threefold παρέδωκεν αὐτοὺς ὁ θεὸς . . . εἰς ἀκαθαρσίαν (i. 24) . . . εἰς πάθη ἀτιμίας (i. 26) · . . εἰς ἀδόκιμον νοῦν (i. 28) to pass, if he had found these words in the text he was using. So it was perhaps hardly to be expected that Harnack would consider very seriously the alternative possibility, that in this case Marcion was unconscious of omitting anything, and did not in fact reject this passage, but merely copied out what he saw in the text he was using. But it is rather surprising that Harnack should have failed, as he evidently did fail, to notice that, while the reasons he gave for Marcion's erasure of this passage might have applied to i. 19-32, they most certainly do not apply to ii. 1. "Wherefore thou art without excuse, O man, whosoever thou art that judgest: for wherein thou judgest the other, thou condemnest thyself; for thou that judgest dost practise the same things." For on Harnack's own showing (*M.* p. 194*) Marcion included in his Gospel the words "judge not that ye be not judged, condemn not that ye be not condemned" (Luke vi. 37, Tert. *Adv. Marc.* IV. 17 'Nolite iudicare, ne iudicemini. Nolite condemnare, ne condemnemini.'). So there is nothing in this verse to which Marcion could or did object. Yet it was as certainly missing in the Apostolicon as the fourteen verses preceding it. What we need, and do not find in Harnack, is some clear explanation of the reason why not only i. 19-32 but the whole passage i. 19-ii. 1 had no place in Marcion's Apostolicon. Such an explanation, and the only one that to my mind accounts quite simply and convincingly for the relevant facts, is that this passage had no place in the text of Romans used by Marcion, being an interpolation added by some scribe writing not in Rome but probably in Ephesus, and belonging to the same circle of Paulinist Christians as the author of the Pastorals. Verse ii. 1 was thus intended by its author to serve as a link connecting i. 19-32 with ii. 2 f. Note the repetition of ὦ ἄνθρωπε ὁ κρίνων.

According to Couchoud the whole of this half chapter i. 19-ii. 1 beginning with διότι, is 'un développement de rhétorique sur l'idolatrie. (Les païens connaissent Dieu, mais ils ont honoré la créature à la place du Créateur. Aussi Dieu les a livrés à la pédérastie, au sapphisme, à tous les vices). Ce hors-d'oeuvre assez plat n'a pas d'accent spécialement paulinien. C'est un lieu commun de diatribe stoïcienne accommodée à la juive . . . Intermède de banalités dans une strophe de haut vol.

'Il est invraisemble que Marcion, s'il a eu sous les yeux les deux pages bigarrées que nous lisons ait pu, avec son éponge et son grattoir, en tirer sept lignes fortes et nues, bien liées et bien sonnantes . . .

Il faut donc laisser (Paul n'y perdra rien) la seconde moitié du chapitre I de *Romains* à l'éditeur catholique'.

Like Harnack and others Couchou seems to forget all about

81

ii. 1 when he is describing i. 19-32.

Though we do not share his extremely disparaging view of this passage, we must admit that it does seem strange and unlike the real Paul to dwell at such length on the ugliest and most unsavoury aspects of paganism just here at the outset of his letter to a church not founded by himself, in the imperial city, where he had never yet set foot.

We too may find it hard to believe that Marcion had these verses before him when he was composing his Apostolicon.

I feel sure Couchoud was right in regarding this passage as an interpolation, but that the evidence now available, especially the linguistic evidence, points to a date much earlier than he allowed.

This same hypothesis is indeed the only one that seems to account for certain lexical data which we must now examine closely. Here in a single page of W.H. we find no fewer than sixteen different words (or including repetitions 19) which do not occur anywhere else in the New Testament. (*P.P.E.* p. 104 f. C1) – καθοράω, θειότης, ἀναπολόγητος 2, ματαιόομαι, μεταλλάσσω 2, σεβάζομαι, χρῆσις 2, ἐκκαίομαι, ὄρεξις, κακοήθεια, ψιθυριστής, κατάλαλος, θεοστυγής, ἐφευρετής, ἀσύνθετος, ἀνελεήμων. Also in the New Testament, but not in any Pauline are nine more (C2) – γνωστός, ἀΐδιος, φάσκω, πετεινός, τετράπους, ἑρπετός, φυσικός, ἀσχημοσύνη, καθήκω. Shared exclusively with the Pastorals are three more (B1) – ὑβριστής, ἀλαζών, ἄστοργος, (also the term γονεῦσιν ἀπειθεῖς). Shared with the Pastorals and other New Testament books are two (B2) – ὑπερήφανος, ἀπειθής. Total nowhere else in Paul (C1+C2+B1+B2) thirty. In the remaining twenty five pages of Romans but nowhere else in Paul we find

C1 nowhere else in the New Testament ..	87 or 3·48 per page. Rom. i. 19-ii. 1				16
C2 in the New Testament, not Pastorals ..	116 „ 4·64 „	„	„	„	9
B1 only in the Pastorals ..	7 „ ·28 „	„	„	„	3

B2 in the New Testament also in Pastorals	21	„	·84	„	„	„	„	2
Total ..	231	„	9·24	„	„	„	„	30

So this page has more than three times as many words which do not occur elsewhere in the Paulines as the remaining twenty five pages of Romans have on the average. Of these it shares with the Pastorals five or more than four times as many as they do on the average, and it shares with the Pastorals exclusively three or more than ten times as many as they do on the average.

Here too we find that fondness for words beginning with a – privative (*P.P.E.* pp. 44, 155 f.) carried to still greater lengths than in the Pastorals. Of the forty eight in Romans seventeen are on this page – C1 ἀναπολόγητος 2, ἀνελεήμων, ἀσύνθετος, C2 ἀΐδιος, ἀσχημοσύνη, ἀτιμάζω, ἀσύνετος, ἀκαθαρσία, B1 ἄστοργος, ἀτίμια, B2 ἀόρατος, ἄφθαρτος, ἀδικία, ἀδόκιμος, ἀπειθής, ἀσέβεια – ἀλήθεια being in both lists. In the remaining twenty five pages of Romans there are thirty two (including ἀλήθεια) or 1.28 per page, in the ten Paulines between 1·5 per page (Galatians) and 2·3 per page (2 Thessalonians). The average per page in 1 Timothy is 4·1, in 2 Timothy 5·1, in Titus 6·75. In the genuine notes embodied in 2 Timothy and Titus there are three, i.e. 1·8 per page.

Most of these lexical data are now published, so far as I know, for the first time, though in 1936 I mentioned a few of them all too briefly in my book about Polycarp[1] as reasons for doubting the Pauline authorship of this passage, and three years later Philip Carrington, then Bishop (later Archbishop) of Quebec, reviewing my book on the Pastoral Epistles[2], pointed out that, when the vocabulary of Rom. i. 18-32 is subjected to the same analysis as I had used in the case of the Pastorals, this passage yields similar results. He

[1]Polycarp's *Two Epistles to the Philippians*, Cambridge, 1936, p. 298.
[2]*Anglican Theological Review* XXI, 1, January 1939.

went on to say that all who, like himself, find my arguments sufficient to disprove the Pauline authorship of the Pastorals, must conclude that Paul did not write 'this apocalypse of God's wrath,' and added 'Nor, in my opinion, did he. He seems to have lifted it from somewhere.'

Bishop Carrington's approval of my book is naturally most encouraging, and so is the fact that his application of my methods to Rom. i. 18-32 has led him to a conclusion so similar to my own. But, with all due respect, I cannot see St. Paul lifting a passage like this from anywhere. As Carrington himself says, the vocabulary and tone of these verses 'agree with the foreign passages in 1 Timothy'. Indeed, as we have seen, they share with the Pastorals enough to indicate a date, like theirs, long after Paul was dead.

A more recent variation on Harnack's solution of this problem is that of E. C. Blackman in *Marcion and his Influence*, London, 1948, p. 45. 'In Rom. i. 16 Marcion removed πρῶτον after 'Ιουδαίῳ, and i. 18 θεοῦ after ὀργή – the good God cannot be angry! The rest of this chapter was omitted *in toto*, doubtless because God is said to have given men over to crimes as a punishment.' It would be interesting to know why Blackman does not even mention Romans ii. 1 in this or in any connexion.

It has long been realized that a literary connexion exists between the last four verses of Romans i and 1 Clem. XXXV. 5, 6, and it has naturally been taken for granted that Clement is here echoing St. Paul. So Lightfoot in his monumental edition of the Apostolic Fathers, Part I, Vol. II, London, 1890, p. 108, comments on πᾶσαν ἀδικίαν κ.τ.λ. 'The whole passage which follows is a reminiscence of Romans i. 29 sq . . .' So too A. J. Carlyle in *The New Testament in the Apostolic Fathers,* by a Committee of the Oxford Society of Historical Theology, Oxford 1905, p. 37 f., 'An examination of this passage makes it practically certain that Clement is influenced by the recollection of the passage in the Epistle to the Romans . . . it would be very difficult to imagine that Clement is here independent of St. Paul.' But it now seems clear that it must be our interpolator who was influenced by his recollection of the passage in 1 Clement. 'That the genuine

Epistle of Clement to the Corinthians was widely known and highly esteemed from the earliest date' we learnt long ago from Lightfoot himself (Op. cit. Vol. I, p. 366). This is surely a striking example of the influence which that Epistle, though never regarded as canonical, certainly exercised in those days.

Neither the interpolator himself nor any other ancient writer can have been aware of the lexical data now pointed out. For neither the critical apparatus nor the interest in such matters requisite for their detection existed in those days – which makes them all the more significant for our present inquiry. His motive can only have been to bring out what he and his readers believed to have been sound Christian doctrine, as well as the mind of the Apostle, on the moral issues involved. Seeing that it has been accepted and expounded as such by orthodox commentators and interpreters through the centuries, it seems clear that he was right in this belief.

CHAPTER IX

ROMANS XVI

It is now getting on for two hundred years since doubts were raised by Keggermann, *De duplici epistolae ad Romanos append-ice*, 1767, as to whether this chapter xvi can really have been addressed to the church at Rome. That it is part of an entirely different letter sent by Paul to the church at Ephesus, as David Schultz maintained in *Theol. Studien und Kritiken*, 1829, p.p. 609 ff, has been accepted by an ever increasing number of experts as the most plausible explanation of the relevant facts. Among the friends greeted by St. Paul and those with him are, first, Prisca and Aquila and the church in their house. Banished from Rome by Claudius in A.D. 52 (Acts xviii. 2), they were with Paul at Ephesus when he wrote 1 Corinthians – for they and the church in their house send greetings to the recipients of that Epistle (xvi. 19) – and they were still (or back?) at Ephesus when Paul wrote his Last Letter (2 Tim. iv. 19). Then Epaenetus the first convert to Christianity in Asia (so P⁴⁶ ABD*G etc., certainly not Achaia), and Mary, 'who worked hard for you' (not 'us'), and a host of other friends, including Rufus and 'his mother and mine' – perhaps the widow of Simon of Cyrene, 'the father of Alexander and Rufus,' who carried the Cross to Golgotha (Mark xv. 21) – certainly an elderly Christian woman in whose house Paul was so much at home that he called her 'Mother.'

Can all this be explained by taking into account the known facilities for travel in those days, and the stream of traffic between the Metropolis and other parts of the Empire – notably Ephesus? Possibly Yes, as Moffatt says, 'in the abstract . . . But the point is that, when Paul wrote Romans, no such migration had occurred. All evidence for it is awant-ing, and the probabilities are against such a wholesale influx of Paul's friends to the capital' (*I.L.N.T.*, 1911, p. 137).

It is true that nearly all the names in Romans xvi. 3-16 appear in the Corpus Inscriptionum Latinarum, many of them belonging to members of the Imperial household during the reign of Nero, as was pointed out by Lightfoot in his famous passage on Caesar's Household (*Philippians,* 1894, pp. 171-8). But it does not by any means follow that the persons bearing these names mentioned by inscriptions in the Catacombs and other early Christian funereal monuments in Rome are the same persons as those mentioned here by St. Paul. As Lightfoot says (p. 171) "In Rome itself, if we may judge by these inscriptions, the 'domus Augusta' must have formed no inconsiderable portion of the whole population" . . . "even with the rarer names the identification must be held highly precarious" (p. 177). Similarly Sanday and Headlam (*Romans,* p. xciv) "It does not prove, of course, that these are the persons to whom the Epistle was written." In no single case is it claimed either by Lightfoot or by Sanday and Headlam that identity of persons is fully established. But even if it were, it would still remain to be proved that these friends of St. Paul were already in Rome when he wrote Romans xvi. Why could they not have gone there after he had written this letter, or after he himself had arrived, or after he had been martyred? Did that movement towards Rome referred to above stop directly the last greetings to Nereus, Olympas &c. had been penned? For no other place in the world have we anything like the vast quantity of materials from which to sift out the wanted names, that we have for the Rome of that age. The only reason why the occurrence of these particular names, among countless others, in the lists of Caesar's Household has been regarded as significant is because in our oldest and best MSS 'chapter xvi' is attached to 'chapters i-xv', and these were undoubtedly addressed and sent to the church at Rome.

So the real question is How did a letter to Paul's friends at Ephesus come to be attached to his letter to the church at Rome? Many have found it easier to believe that this happened through some mistake by a copyist than to follow Sanday and Headlam's Commentary, or that of Dodd (in Moffatt's *N.T. Comm.,* 1932), in the old dubious assumption that all these friends of the Apostle had migrated en masse to Rome before this Epistle was written.

But there is still another possibility, which I have long believed to be the true solution of this problem. It is that when Paul dictated Romans at Corinth, before leaving that city for his last journey to Jerusalem via Philippi and Troas, he asked his friend and amanuensis Tertius to make a second copy of this, the fullest and most systematic statement of his central beliefs he ever committed to writing, for the church at Ephesus, where he had spent nearly three years, and where he had many friends by whom what he had written would be read with deeper interest and understanding than by anyone in Rome. For they had heard from his own lips the discussions and expositions of which this Epistle is a sort of summary and record. Phoebe, the deaconess of the church at Cenchreae, was going to Ephesus, and had asked him to give her an introduction to people there who would help her and perhaps provide her with the hospitality she needed. Our 'chapter xvi' is the postcript added for this purpose to the Ephesian copy of 'chapters i-xv' which she carried with her. While he was about it, Paul naturally took the opportunity to send greetings from himself and those with him who, like himself, had many friends in Ephesus, but few if any in Rome. At the same time he added the warning against mischief-makers, of whose activities he was only too well aware (vs. 17 f.), and the assurance of his confidence in the loyalty of his readers (vs. 19), which come so much more naturally from him in a message to Ephesus than in one to Rome, where he had never yet set foot.

So when the first collection of Paul's letters was made at Ephesus *c.* A.D. 90, (see above, Chapter VI), those who made it did not need to apply to Rome for a copy of this letter, because they had their own copy. Naturally they used that, including the postscript, which was not a separate covering note but an integral part of the letter as it reached Ephesus. (Note the δὲ in vs. 1). Thus the addition of this chapter was not due to any mistake, but was made by the express wish of Paul himself.

As long ago as the spring of 1929 I expounded this view of

the matter to my friend B. H. Streeter in a communication on 'The Date of the Pastorals' of which I have kept a copy. Later in that same year Streeter published his book on 'The Primitive Church', with the note (p. 103) – 'Personally I accept the view that Romans xvi was originally a separate letter to the church at Ephesus, or else a postscript appended to a copy of Romans sent by Paul himself to the Ephesians at the time of writing.' That is the earliest appearance of this view in print known to me.

The only objection to it, surely, was pointed out long ago by C. R. Gregory in his *Canon and Text of the New Testament*, Edinburgh, 1907, p. 524, 'If, however, this letter, that is to say, this sixteenth chapter in the main, had been written to Ephesus, and if that fact were to be reflected in the documents which contain the text, the doxology would not be moved from the end of the sixteenth chapter to the end of the fourteenth, but to the end of the fifteenth chapter. But no single document puts the doxology there.'

That is exactly where our earliest copy of Romans, the Chester Beatty Codex P⁴⁶, does put it.

The text of this important discovery was made available by Sir Frederic Kenyon in *The Chester Beatty Biblical Papyri Descriptions and Text of Twelve Manuscripts on Papyrus of the Greek Bible, Fasciculus III Supplement Pauline Epistles*, London 1936.' In that same year I inserted into my book on 'Polycarp's Two Epistles . . .' (p. 22, n, 1) a brief footnote on the new support here given to my theory about Romans xvi. (My first impression that this reading occurs in *several* manuscripts was a bad mistake. For 'in some MSS' I should of course have written 'in one MS, P⁴⁶').

In 1946 I argued at some length for this view of Romans xvi in a chapter on 'Erastus and his Ledger' (pp. 16-21) of which copies were sent to a score or so of my friends, including T. W. Manson.

Two years later Manson himself sent me a copy of his article on 'St. Paul's Letter to the Romans – and others', reprinted from the *Bulletin of the John Rylands Library*, Vol. 31, No. 2, November 1948 (Manchester University Press). Here with characteristic learning and ability he showed himself a doughty champion of the same view.

In the *Harvard Theological Review*, Vol. XLIV, No. 1, January 1951, pp. 55-57 Edgar J. Goodspeed mentions Manson's article, but seems to prefer the view that Romans xvi is an entirely different letter from i-xv. He calls it 'Phoebe's Letter of Introduction', and dwells on the difficulties and dangers besetting a woman who travelled alone in those days, and stresses her need, on her arrival in Ephesus, for such help, including hospitality, as the friends named would be sure to give her. Goodspeed holds that when the first Corpus Paulinum was made, as he has long sought to show, at Ephesus, 'it would be very natural to include this letter as an appendix to the great letter to Rome, written from the same place at the same time' – omitting only its opening salutation (as when 2 Corinthians x-xiii was combined with 2 Corinthians i-ix). He finds strong confirmation of this view in the place given by P⁴⁶ to the Doxology.

This is certainly far better than the old view held by conservatively minded scholars who cling to 'tradition' as represented by the majority of MSS, but ignore, or had not yet heard of, the earlier tradition reflected in our oldest MS of Romans. But all that Goodspeed says in support of Schultz's hypothesis can equally well be said of the view advocated by Manson and myself. Why Goodspeed prefers Schultz's view to ours he does not say, nor can I imagine. Nor can I agree that the analogy of 2 Corinthians x-xiii helps him. For we have no evidence whatever to show that the loss of its opening salutation is the only loss this 'Four-chapter-letter' has suffered, as he assumes. On the contrary it is certain that no other letter of Paul's has come down to us with a δέ in the first sentence after its opening salutation. Romans itself has in i. 8 not δέ but πρῶτον μέν. In the original copy of this Epistle as it reached Ephesus, on our theory, 'chapter xvi' followed immediately after xv. 33.

Of the Doxology, xvi. 25 ff., Harnack wrote, 'Marcion did not present these verses, and did not know them, but they are obviously Marcionite, and only laboriously and inadequately catholicized by two or three additions.' As Catholic additions Harnack specified καὶ τὸ κήρυγμα 'Ιησοῦ Χριστοῦ . . .

διά τε γραφῶν προφητικῶν, . . . and γνωρισθέντες- (Marcion, Leipzig, 1924², p. 165*). For Harnack's earlier discussion of this matter see the Sitzungsbericht der Preuss. Akad. d. Wissenschaft 1919, p. 527 ff., where the Marcionite character of these verses and the assumption of Catholic interpolations are thoroughly and precisely grounded.

CHAPTER X

PHILIPPIANS AND 2 TIMOTHY

It has long been widely recognized as a highly significant fact that St. Paul uses the same series of striking metaphors twice to describe the situation in which he finds himself at the time of writing, first in Philippians and then again in 2 Timothy, but in each case with this difference – what in Philippians was a future possibility, which might or might not turn out as then seemed likely, in 2 Timothy has either happened already or is on the point of doing so. The issue, then still open, is now closed.

Thus in Philippians ii. 17 he says 'even if my life blood is to be poured out on the altar' . . . (εἰ καὶ σπένδομαι), in 2 Timothy iv. 6 'already my life blood is being poured out on the altar' (ἐγὼ γὰρ ἤδη σπένδομαι). In Philippians iii. 12-14 he is still running the great race, he hopes not in vain (ὅτι οὐκ εἰς κενὸν ἔδραμον, ii. 16), with eyes set on the mark, but not yet within reach of the prize (ἐγὼ ἐμαυτὸν οὔπω λογίζομαι κατειληφέναι, . . . κατὰ σκόπον διώκω εἰς τὸ βραβεῖον). In 2 Tim. iv. 7 f. the race is over and it only remains for him to go and receive his crown (τὸν δρόμον τετέλεκα, . . . λοιπὸν ἀπόκειταί μοι ὁ στέφανος). In Phil. i. 27, 30, iv. 3 he and his fellow-athletes are still engaged in the fight, or contest, of life (συναθλοῦντες, . . . τὸν αὐτὸν ἀγῶνα ἔχοντες, . . . οἵτινες συνήθλησάν μοι). In 2 Tim. iv. 7 he has fought the good fight (τὸν καλὸν ἀγῶνα ἠγώνισμαι). In Phil. iv. 13 nothing is impossible to Paul 'in Him that strengtheneth me' (ἐν τῷ ἐνδυναμοῦντί με). In 2 Tim. iv. 17 when others forsook him, the Lord stood by him and strengthened him (ὁ δὲ κύριος . . . ἐνεδυνάμωσέν με). In Phil. i. 23 he longs for the time to come when he will be able to cut loose his moorings, or weigh anchor, and put out to sea (τὴν ἐπιθυμίαν ἔχων εἰς τὸ ἀναλῦσαι . . .). In 2 Tim. iv. 6 the time has come, and the moment of his departure is at hand (ὁ καιρὸς τῆς ἀναλύσεώς μου ἐφέστηκεν).

All these verses in 2 Timothy echo those in Philippians, and must have been written fairly soon after that Epistle. But the vital question still remains, where and when were they written?

I

In 1921 (*P.P.E.* p. 112 f.) I tried to show that Philippians was in fact written towards the end of Paul's one and only Roman imprisonment, and (pp. 126-134) his 'Last Letter', including all the verses quoted above from 2 Timothy except iv. 17 – I have long included this verse too – at the end of that imprisonment, on the eve, or perhaps on the very day, of his martyrdom. For my final distribution of the genuine matter in 2 Timothy see my article in *The Expository Times*, Dec. 1955 – (a) 'Last Letter', i. 16-18, iii. 10, 11, iv. 1. 2a, 5b-8, 16-19, P.S. and Benediction 21b, 22a, (b) an earlier note, soon after Paul left Ephesus for the last time, iv. 9-15, P.S. and Benediction, 20, 21a, 22b.

II

A very different view is that proposed by Dr. G. S. Duncan in his book *Saint Paul's Ephesian Ministry* (London, 1929, later cited by him as *S.P.E.M.*), in which he argues that not only all the four 'prison letters', Ephesians, Philippians, Colossians and Philemon, but also all the genuine 'fragments' in 2 Timothy, were written inside Paul's Ephesian period, during various imprisonments not recorded in Acts – Philippians before 1 Corinthians in Ephesus itself, Colossians, Philemon, (and Ephesians, if genuine, as he believes it to be), also in Ephesus, but later than 1 Corinthians, and the 'fragments' in 2 Timothy, including i. 15-18, elsewhere in Asia, probably at Laodicea. This last is of course only possible if he is right in substituting ἐν Λαοδικείᾳ for ἐν Ῥώμῃ in i. 17. As corroborative evidence in support of this textual change he refers to a note at the end of 1 and 2 Timothy in Codex A and in the Coptic Versions assigning both these Epistles to Laodicea.

With Duncan's reconstruction as a whole few if any have, so far as I know, signified their agreement. But the number

93

of scholars who have adopted one part of it or another must be very considerable.

As already indicated, I am one of many who cannot believe that St. Paul wrote Ephesians either at Ephesus or anywhere else, but thanks to Duncan I am fully convinced that Paul wrote Philemon and the letter he sent with it to the church at Colossae during a brief period of house-arrest (*libera custodia*) at Ephesus.

My objections to Duncan's argument about Philippians and the genuine matter in 2 Timothy were stated in an article not intended for publication, but sent in the first instance to him, then to a few friends, and later printed in *N.T.S.*, Vol. 2, No. 4, May 1956. His 'Brief Postscript' by way of reply in *N.T.S.*, Vol. 3, No. 3, May 1957 ended with the words 'Harrison's objections with regard to Philippians leave me wholly unmoved.'

His Chronological Table in *N.T.S.*, Vol. 5, No. 1, Oct. 1958 brings out points at which he has modified his earlier position. Otherwise, we gather, he is of the same mind as in 1929.

He and I are agreed that, while 2 Timothy as a whole cannot possibly be the first-hand work of St. Paul, certain verses in it belong to a genuine note sent by the real Paul to the real Timothy not long after he had written Philippians. He too finds in this genuine note 'echoes' from Philippians, with the difference that 'Paul's situation', which in Philippians was already 'serious', in 2 Timothy 'has grown critical in the extreme, he catches up the figurative expressions of the earlier letter, and by a series of perfect tenses emphasizes that what were then seen as possibilities have now become dire actualities . . . Here surely we have an authentic echo of the voice that sounds in Phililpians . . . and the interval which separates sound and echo cannot be great' (*S.P.E.M.* p. 190).

But there our agreement ends. He is as sure as ever that Philippians was written at Ephesus. I am equally sure that it was written in Rome. He still regards it as probable that all the genuine verses in 2 Timothy belong to the same note, written perhaps at Laodicea. I am fully convinced that they form two different notes, one written in Rome, the other perhaps at Nicopolis, certainly soon after Paul left Ephesus for the last time.

III

It is evident that here, on an issue of no small importance for students of the New Testament, our two interpretations of the relevant data are mutually contradictory and irreconcilable. So it is now for other scholars to decide which of us (if either) they think is right.

1. It is surely high time that any doubts raised by Duncan about the reading ἐν ʿΡώμῃ in 2 Tim. i. 17 were either confirmed or silenced once and for all. In his latest reference to this matter (*N. T.S.*, Vol. 3, No. 3, May 1957, p. 218), though he sees that ʿwhat is said in i. 16-18 about Onesiphorus' presence in Rome must of course belong to a later period, if the statement in this form comes from the pen of the apostle,' he still regards it as 'probable that all the personal passages in 2 Timothy come from the Ephesian period.' This, he tells us is not a *necessary* part of his thesis, even if he did 'venture to raise doubts about the reading ἐν ʿΡώμῃ, recalling the evidence of Codex A and the Coptic Versions for associating the letter with Laodicea rather than with Rome.'

But on his own showing (*S.P.E.M.* p. 198), what the brief notes appended to these documents actually state is that 2 Timothy (as well as 1 Timothy) was written at Laodicea. No one today believes that statement to be true; and even if it were true, this would not make it any more likely than it was before that the genuine note, which Duncan and I agree is embodied in 2 Timothy, was also written at Laodicea. So what he calls 'evidence', and uses to corroborate his own conjecture, is nothing more than a dubious inference from an erroneous statement in a few obviously unreliable subscriptions, whereas the reading ἐν ʿΡώμῃ is accepted by all editors of the Greek Testament, vouched for by every Greek MS containing this Epistle, including Codex A itself, and supported by a mass of subsidiary attestation.

2. Do Paul's own words in 2 Tim. iv. 6-8 mean that at the time of writing he sees his own death as imminent and certain? I say Yes. Duncan in his book says, 'It has been far

too readily assumed that verses 6-8 necessarily imply that the apostle is facing the prospect of almost immediate death. . . . Paul is able to look facts in the face and to recognize that, baulked as his enemies have been on this occasion, they will some day succeed in bringing him to his death' (*S.P.E.M.* p. 210).

But '*some day*' etc. here involves either a mistranslation or a substitution of some quite different words for those actually used by the Apostle. Neither in our Authorised Version nor in the Revised nor in the New English Bible can support be found for any such interpretation of this passage.

Since reading my comment in *N.T.S.*, May 1956, p. 255, Duncan seems to halt between two opinions, and his approach is more 'tentative' than ever. In *N.T.S.*, May 1957, p. 213 he writes 'II Tim. iv. 6-22 is of special significance for our inquiry. . . . In vv 6-8 (if they are an integral part of the passage) he is resigned to death. But by divine help he has been rescued as from the lion's mouth, and he is convinced that he will now be spared to resume the work of world-evangelization.'

Either these verses are an integral part of this passage, or else they are not. Does either of these two ways of escape for Duncan meet the case?

(1) Let us take it first that he still 'eschews the over-easy solution of dividing up the note into separate fragments' (*S.P.E.M.* p. 208). In that case the death to which Paul is resigned is not coming today, nor tomorrow, nor next week, but *some day* in the quite indefinite future. Meanwhile he is looking forward confidently to another spell of missionary activity. To all intents and purposes this is merely a repetition of the original error in *S.P.E.M.* p. 210, and is open to the same fatal objection,– it conflicts with the plain meaning of ἤδη σπένδομαι, ἐφέστηκεν and the series of perfect tenses to which Duncan himself drew attention thirty five years ago.

(2) His other way of escape appears on p. 217 f. of the same issue (*N.T.S.*, May 1957). 'The prospect of death in vv. 6-8 seems to be in violent contrast with the assurance of deliverance, and the confident outlook on the future, in the verses which follow. But the contrast corresponds precisely to what,

in retrospect, Paul writes in II Cor. i. 8 ff., and if the two passages are to be separated, it need not be by a long interval, and the reference in both may be to the same awesome experience.' By this Duncan clearly means the 'thirty-nine stripes' (II Cor. xi. 24) which 'he was made to suffer' by 'a purely ecclesiastical court' at Laodicea, where 'the Jews of Asia . . . now saw their opportunity to take the law into their own hands . . . and flogging . . . might well have brought him to the verge of death' (Op. cit. p. 215).

Let us assume, for the sake of the argument, that this hypothetical reconstruction is a correct account of what actually happened in Asia. Before such a tribunal it might have been futile for Paul to assert his Roman citizenship; and he would not be the only man who has recovered after being flogged within an inch of his life. When he looked back on it, one can imagine him writing as he did in 2 Cor. i. 8 ff. What I cannot imagine and cannot believe, is that it was there and then he wrote 2 Tim. iv. 6-22 either all at once or first 6-8 and then, not long afterwards, the rest of that chapter.

There is indeed a transition, (I should not call it a violent contrast), from the thought of imminent death in vv. 6, 7 to the confident assurance in 16-18 that his Lord will bring him safely through to His heavenly kingdom, there to receive the crown laid up for all who have loved His appearing (vs. 8). But so far from corresponding precisely to what Paul writes in 2 Cor. i. 8 ff., the two are poles apart. 'We were weighed down exceedingly beyond our power, insomuch that we despaired even of life.' These are the words Paul chose to describe the state of mind to which he had been reduced by the affliction that befell him in Asia. Such were the depths to which, by his own confession, the sheer physical torture he then suffered had brought him down, and from which he had been raised as it were from the dead.

But is what he writes in 2 Tim. iv. 6-8 the language of despair? 'I have fought the good fight, I have finished the course, I have kept the faith, henceforth . . .' are these the accents of despair? No, ἐξαπορηθῆναι was the best word he could find to let his friends in Corinth know what that

97

affliction in Asia had done to his spirit. Of all the perils and narrow escapes through which he had passed, this was the only time he had quite given up hope. Never before and never again in his letters do we find such an admission. When he wrote 2 Cor. iv. 8 he was still hard pressed on every side, still persecuted, still perplexed, but no longer desperate (οὐκ ἐξαπορούμενοι). Paul the dauntless was himself again.

But when he wanted to let Timothy know in what frame of mind he was facing the greatest crisis of all, when he did not only *think* he was going to die, but knew beyond all peradventure that the hour of his longed for departure from this world had come, and that he would soon be with Christ, which was 'very far better', could any word be found less fitted than 'despair' to express what he actually felt and wrote?

3. To show how wrong we are in 'connecting that critical hour when the aspostle had to face examination with no one to stand by him (iv. 16) with his formal trial at Rome,' Duncan asks, 'Would Paul, knowing that such a trial was to take place, have sent off everyone of his lieutenants on their travels, and then emphasized the fact that his only companion now was Luke?' (*N.T.S.*, May 1957, p. 218).

Duncan himself holds that iv. 11 'only Luke is with me' was written in A.D. 55 (*S.P.E.M.* p. 298 f.) and he knows that I say it was written in A.D. 56. For he has just mentioned this twice, first on the previous page, and again on this same page 218, line 5. So this question is merely a slip on his part, and needs no answer.

4. Yet another point of difference between us is, how long an interval can we resonably allow between the 'sound' of these striking metaphors in Philippians and the 'echoes' in 2 Timothy iv. 6-22?

On page 298 of *S.P.E.M.* he made it well over a year, from summer 54 to autumn 55. On his latest showing (*N.T.S.*, Oct. 1958, p. 43) it was all or most of a year, from autumn 54 or early 55 to autumn 55 – and every one of these months crowded to capacity with a multitude of conflicting demands on his time and attention. Duncan himself regards the whole Ephesian period as a 'boisterous' one of 'great literary activity' (*S.P.E.M.*, p. 297). It certainly was a time of unceasing strain and stress, marked by 'the daily onslaught of his missionary duties' (l, c, p. 295), which had to be done in the teeth of 'violent efforts to undermine his teaching and authority' (*N.T.S.* May 1957, p. 218) made by his enemies at Ephesus, that 'power house of opposition,' and elsewhere (*S.P.E.M.* p. 29). His 'anxiety for all the churches', which pressed upon him daily (2 Cor. xi. 28), must have reached its climax when, torn in two between the rival claims of two great centres, he was forced, against his will and against his better judgement, to make that hurried and, as it turned out, futile journey to Corinth – the 'sorrowful visit' – and finally, if Duncan is right, yet another journey, this time to the Lycus valley.

Is it really likely, or even credible, that through all these hectic months, and amid all these distractions, he was able to keep that whole series of metaphors so firmly fixed in his mind that, at the end of it all, he could reproduce them one after another without an omission and without a mistake?

My own account makes the intervening period between Philippians and Paul's 'Last Letter' at most a few weeks, and these were spent in prison, where one day was very much like another, with plenty of time for reminiscence and reflection, and apart from his recent 'first defence' nothing happened that we know of in any way calculated to make him forget what he had written to those dear friends at Philippi, whom he knew by this time that he would never see on earth again.

CHAPTER XI

ERASTUS AND HIS PAVEMENT

On April 15, 1929 a stone was discovered in Corinth bearing this inscription

ERASTVS . PRO.AED.
S.P. STRAVIT

This was taken by the American excavators who found it[1] to represent 'Erastus Procurator (=Steward) Aedile laid this pavement at his own expense (Sua Pecunia)'.

The inscription was dated by some experts in ancient letter-formation early in the second century, by others in the second half of the first century. The pavement was repaired *c.* A.D. 150, and the inscribed stone was then removed from its original place, and laid down with the stones forming the pavement. This would hardly be done while the donor was alive, nor would the pavement be likely to need repairing soon after it was first laid. So if those experts who favour the earlier date are right, as they may very well be, and the pavement was laid say about A.D. 75–80, there would seem to be a primâ facie case for identifying this Erastus with Paul's friend. Not unnaturally the discoverers and others thought so.

But then Dr. H. J. Cadbury, in a very thorough examination of this matter,[2] insisted that 'the identity of the three Erasti in the New Testament . . . is not certain and must not be finally assumed', and challenged the interpretation of the letters PRO as = PROCURATOR, pointing out that the usual abbreviation of PROCURATOR is not PRO but

---

[1]See (a) 'Excavations in the Theatre District and Tombs of Corinth in 1929' by T. L. Shear, in *The American Journal of Archæology*, 2nd Series, Vol. xxxiii, p. 325 f. (with photograph), 1929; (b) *L'Année Épigraphique*, No. 118, 1930.

[2]*Journal of Biblical Literature*, Vol. I, Part ii, pp. 42–58, 1931.

PROC. He maintained that PRO AED stands for PRO AEDILITATE – itself an abbreviation for the more usual PRO HONORE or OB HONOREM AEDILITATIS, as proposed by Professor Roos of Leiden – and means 'in return for the honour of the office of aedile'. On the status and functions of an οἰκονόμος τῆς πόλεως Dr. Cadbury pointed out that the term occurs nowhere else in literature, but appears in numerous inscriptions, and stressed the importance of Peter Landvogt's monograph, *Epigraphische Untersuchungen über den οἰκονόμος*, Strassbourg 1908, where it seems to be established that this official lost under the Romans most of the social status and financial authority held by his predecessors in the Hellenistic period. Assuming that Paul's friend was still a slave when he became οἰκονόμος τῆς πόλεως at Corinth, and equating this office with *arcarius rei publicae*, he concluded that 'the identification of the Erastus of the inscription with a New Testament character is improbable if not impossible. . . . What makes it seem impossible is the difficulty of supposing that any man's *cursus honorum* included both *arcarius rei publicae* and *aedile*.'

If, in face of this weighty judgement, I venture to suggest that there is still much to be said for the identification of Paul's friend with the Erastus of the pavement, and that this intensely interesting possibility may not after all be so remote as Dr. Cadbury felt bound to suppose, I do so with the deference due to so great an authority.

I think it can be shown (a) that Erastus in Rom. xvi. 23 is the same person as in 2 Tim. iv. 20 and Acts xix. 22; (b) that he was already a freedman when he reached Corinth; (c) that his new post, though certainly not (as in the Revised Version and in the New English Bible) the city treasurership, was much the most important of its kind in Greece; (d) that it would only have been given to a man of quite exceptional character and experience as an οἰκονόμος; (e) that a freedman of character and ability could go far in those days; (f) that in all probability PRO AED here stands for PRO AEDILE or PRO AEDILIS, meaning deputy or vice- aedile during the temporary absence of the aedile; (g) that after Erastus had served for twenty years or so as οἰκονόμος τῆς πόλεως or

101

clerk of the works under the aedile (superintendent of public works) at Corinth, it would not have been easy to find anyone else half so well qualified as he must have been to carry on during some temporary absence of his chief; (h) that his temporary appointment in such circumstances is much more likely than that when he was still clerk of the works a vacancy in the aedileship was filled by appointing to that office another man also named Erastus.

1. In the first place, then, now that the evidence of the Chester Beatty Codex P⁴⁶ has removed the only real difficulty in the widely held conviction that Rom. xvi was addressed to Ephesus, (see above, Chapter IX), the identity of Erastus who 'stayed on at Corinth' as οἰκονόμος of that city with Erastus whom Paul sent with Timothy from Ephesus into Macedonia becomes just as much a matter of course as the identity of Timothy who in Rom. xvi. 21 sends greetings to Ephesus, with the Timothy whom Paul sent with Erastus from Ephesus into Macedonia, and the Timothy to whom Paul addressed his Last Letter.

2. This makes it practically certain that Erastus must have gained in or near Ephesus the necessary experience of the kind of work he would have to do as οἰκονόμος of Corinth. I do not know how else he could have got such experience, if not as steward of some rich man in Ephesus. As such he had in all probability been a slave. But that he had earned his manumission not, as Dr. Cadbury suggests, at Corinth but at Ephesus, is strongly indicated by the fact that he was able to go on that errand for Paul first to Macedonia and then on to Corinth.

3. I agree with Cadbury that the evidence of Peter Landvogt's inscriptions proves conclusively that an οἰκονόμος of Corinth when Paul wrote Rom. xvi. 23 could not possibly have been the 'treasurer' of that city, but must have been either a slave or a freedman, and his duties not high finance but much humbler jobs under the aedile. Yet even so it must be remembered that Corinth was at that time a Roman colony, capital of the Roman province of Achaia and by far

the biggest, busiest, wealthiest and most important commercial centre in Greece. It follows that in his own line Erastus had now reached the top of the ladder, his new post being much the most important of its kind anywhere in that region.

4. Such a post would not have been given by the authorities responsible for it on any other grounds than proved experience as an οἰκονόμος, and integrity as well as competence shown in his previous post. Erastus can only have won this appointment on his merits.

5. We know that a freedman of exceptional character and ability could go far, and sometimes did so, in those days, e.g. Narcissus, secretary of the Emperor Claudius, 'over whom he possessed unbounded influence' (Smith's *Smaller Classical Dictionary*, London, 1908,[29] p. 389). Dr. Cadbury himself admits that 'an Erastus who was a public slave in the time of Paul might at the time of the inscription have been manumitted and have become aedile of Corinth' (op. cit. p. 55).

6. If we must find a Latin equivalent for οἰκ. τῆς πόλεως, *arcarius civitatis*, as in the Vulgate, or *arcarius rei publicae*, may well meet the case, though, as Landvogt says, 'the Roman designation occurs extremely seldom. Even in the Roman period the designation οἰκονόμος is almost exclusively retained. W. Wilcken (*Ostraka I*, p. 499) traces this back to the fact that in the Roman period the οἰκ. counted as one of the lower posts' (den niederen Chargen. Op. cit. p. 10). We shall not be far out if we regard him as 'clerk of the works', or as Cadbury suggests 'manager'. In this capacity he would almost certainly have slaves working under him in the various tasks which he must supervise under the aedile's instructions. These might include, but would certainly not be confined to, such odd jobs as the memorial pillars and statues mentioned in Landvogt's inscriptions. In all probability they would include repairs to public buildings and highways, for which we know an aedile was always responsible.

7. The standing of Erastus in our inscription will be as clear to us as it must have been to him and his contemporaries, if and when we can be sure that those letters PRO AED, which can only have meant one thing to them, mean the same thing to us. Unfortunately they occur nowhere else

either in our literature or in inscriptions. So we must make do as best we can with the help of analogies.

We can safely rule out at once as analogous abbreviations PRO CONS. and PRO PR., both of which occur frequently enough. The first means a proconsul, 'one who at the close of his consulship at Rome became governor of a province . . .' (Lewis and Short, s.v.). The second was a propraetor, 'a magistrate under the republic who, having administered the praetorship one year in Rome, was sent in the following year as praetor to a province where there was no army'. Whatever else PRO AED may mean, it clearly applies to an official whose sphere is a city, not a province.

But why should it not stand simply for PRO AEDILE or PRO AEDILIS, meaning 'deputy aedile', i.e. 'one who acts for the aedile during the temporary absence of that official', like PRO MAGISTRO or PRO MAGISTER (*Inscr. Fabr.* p. 442, 49; *Inscr. Grut.* 426, 5; 607, 1 etc.), 'one who presides, rules, etc. in place of another, a vice-president, vice-gerent, vice-director', and PRO DICTATORE = vice-dictator (Livy 22, 31 fin.)?

In the very nature of things there were bound to be occasions when, for one reason or another, the aedile was unable to attend to his duties, and during his temporary absence somebody must have acted as his deputy. A clerk of the works who over a period of years had proved himself both competent and trustworthy, would obviously be a far better deputy than a person of excellent family connexions and high social status but little or no experience of the multifarious practical tasks for which the aedile was responsible. If such a deputy must not be called, or call himself, PRO AEDILE, I do not know how else to describe him. And if, having saved up enough money, as he may well have done, our Erastus felt moved to celebrate the occasion – and avoid any risk of finding that his use of public money for this purpose did not meet with approval – by having this pavement laid without charge to civic funds, he could hardly express this more simply, briefly and naturally than someone called Erastus has done in this inscription.

I agree that beforehand it might have seemed unlikely to

Paul himself, had he considered it, that his friend would ever attain the full rank of aedile as a permanent appointment. But that is not at all the same thing as for us now to regard it as so very improbable that he may have been called upon to serve as deputy during a temporary absence of the aedile his chief. So far from finding this hard to believe, I should have thought it was more than likely to happen sooner or later to a man like Erastus.

I assume, with Dr. Cadbury, that Paul's friend was still alive, and all his faculties unimpaired, when the inscription was made. Otherwise of course the question as to his identity with the donor of the pavement would not arise.

If it were established that PRO AED can only mean 'in return for the honor of his appointment to the aedileship', I could even believe that, after twenty years or so as clerk of the works, always doing his level best, in accordance with Paul's teaching, 'as unto the Lord and not unto men' (Col. iii. 23), this well-known, zealous and highly efficient public servant (as he must have become by this time), was himself appointed aedile of Corinth. After all, more unlikely things than that have happened.

What I find simply incredible is that, when our Erastus had completed twenty years in his original post at Corinth, the aedileship there, having fallen vacant, was given to another man also named Erastus, so that, by a much too curious coincidence, the new superintendent of public works and his experienced clerk of the works both had the same name.

CHAPTER XII

THREE GENUINE NOTES

(i) Titus iii. 12-15. Paul writes from Western Macedonia, several months after 2 Cor. x-xiii, and before 2 Cor. i-ix, bidding Titus, who is at Corinth, be ready to join him in Epirus.

> When I shall send Artemas unto thee, or Tychicus, give diligence to come unto me to Nicopolis : for there I have determined to winter. Set forward Zenas the lawyer and Apollos on their journey diligently, that nothing be wanting unto them. And let our people also learn to maintain good works for necessary uses, that they be not unfruitful . . .
>
> All that are with me salute thee. Salute them that love us in faith. Grace be with you all.

Some months before Paul left Ephesus for the last time, he explained to the Corinthians[1] his intention to pay them an extended visit, and possibly spend the winter among them, after first passing through Macedonia. Apparently they were expecting him to take Corinth first, on his way to Macedonia, and then again on his way to Jerusalem. But, gladly as he would have given them the double 'benefit' (2 Cor. i. 15), that plan would involve, in the first instance, a hasty visit (ἐν παρόδῳ), which, at the present critical juncture (ἄρτι), he was anxious to avoid. Meanwhile Timothy might be coming, with others, and if so, they must not let any one 'despise' him. Paul had done his utmost to persuade Apollos to join this company; but Apollos declined. He would come, however, on the next convenient opportunity. It was soon made only too clear that the disaffection at Corinth was even more serious than Paul had realized. Certain persons had taken full advantage of their opportunities, while his back was

---

[1] 1 Cor. xvi. 5–12.

turned, to disparage his work and undermine his influence. Much against his will, and to the detriment of urgent claims at Ephesus, he was forced to pay a flying visit to Corinth[2], only to find that he might as well have spared himself the trouble. The time was too short, and the mischief had gone too far. His enemies had not struck without making sure of support. Remarks like those quoted in 2 Cor. x. 10 left him nothing to say, and nothing to do but withdraw. Deeply humiliated, and in great distress of mind, he returned to Ephesus, and wrote the letter mentioned in 2 Cor. ii. 4, vii. 8. With the severity of injured love, it vindicated his good faith and authority. There are strong reasons for believing, with Moffatt (*I.L.N.T.*, 1911, pp. 119-123) and many others, that part of this 'intermediate letter' is preserved in the last four chapters of 2 Corinthians. The jubilant assurance of his restored confidence (vii. 16) could hardly be followed, in one and the same letter, by such expressions of profound distrust as we find, e.g., in xii. 20 f. It was now the turn of Titus to try whether he could succeed, where Timothy and Paul himself had failed. Soon afterwards Paul left Ephesus. For the reason stated in 2 Cor. ii. 1, he took the long northern route, resolved to enter Corinth for the third time, as soon as he could do so happily – i.e., on hearing from Titus of the success of his efforts – but not before ($\mu\grave{\eta}$ $\pi\acute{\alpha}\lambda\iota\nu$ $\grave{\epsilon}\nu$ $\lambda\acute{\upsilon}\pi\eta$). He had some hope of finding Titus at Troas (2 Cor. ii. 12 f.); but this zealous friend had not yet had time to carry out his difficult task; so he missed this conditional appointment. Restless and distraught, Paul could not stay to take the opportunities opening up at Troas, but pushed on into Macedonia. There too he found no relief, but afflictions on every side, fightings without and forebodings within (vii. 5). Yet, undeterred either by outward opposition or by inward misgivings, being the man he was, he still pushed forward, proclaiming his gospel of divine comfort and immortal hope, and pressing on with that collection for the poor at Jerusalem which meant so much to him. We are told in Acts xx. 2 that he made his way 'through those parts'. In its context this can only mean through Macedonia, presumably by the Via Egnatia. At

[2] 2 Cor. xii. 14, xiii. 1 f. ($\tau\rho\acute{\iota}\tau o\nu$ $\tauo\hat{\upsilon}\tauo$) . . . $\grave{\omega}s$ $\pi\alpha\rho\grave{\omega}\nu$ $\tau\grave{o}$ $\delta\epsilon\acute{\upsilon}\tau\epsilon\rho o\nu$,

Dyrrachium we picture him looking out over the Adriatic to where, beyond the western horizon, Rome beckoned. It was now only a step to Illyricum. Thus was realized his dream of 2 Cor. x. 15 f. While that faith, or fidelity, which had waned, was waxing again, he did in fact sow the good seed on virgin soil in 'regions beyond'. That he did not then simply retrace his steps is already suggested by the κύκλῳ in Rom. xv. 19; and this is confirmed, in our view, by the note before us, written about this time.

Paul cannot have written it 'from Nicopolis of Macedonia' – as stated in the old note appended to Titus in the T.R. and A.V., but rightly omitted from the R.V. and all modern texts – even if there was such a place. For if so, he must have written not 'there' (ἐκεῖ) but 'here'. The bearer will have been Artemas, as Tychicus was sent to Ephesus (2 Tim. iv. 12), presumably with note (ii). How Titus kept this appointment, and was able to bring such good news as made up for many things, we read in 2 Cor. i-ix, written at Nicopolis under the great reaction of joy which followed his coming.

We now learn that Apollos had found his convenient opportunity, and was at Corinth, on his way with Zenas to some destination which we have no means of defining more closely. If now, notwithstanding the κέκρικα (Tit. iii. 12), Paul did after all spend that winter at Corinth, he would not this time be accused of having changed his mind too 'lightly' (2 Cor. i. 17).

The diction of this note coincides with that of 1 Cor. xvi at too many points to leave room for doubt that it must have been written after no great interval. ὅταν, πέμψω, πρός σε, (ὑμᾶς), ἤ, ἐλθεῖν πρός με, παραχειμάσαι, ᾿Απολλῶν, πρόπεμψον, ἵνα, μὴ, ἀσπάζονταί σε (ὑμᾶς) . . . οἱ. πάντες, ἄσπασαι τοὺς φιλοῦντας (φιλεῖ), ἡ χάρις . . . μετὰ πάντων ὑμῶν together make a series which can hardly be dismissed as accidental. See further for ἐκεῖ Rom. xv. 24, κέκρικα 1 Cor. v. 3, σπούδασον 2 Cor. viii. 16 f. (σπουδήν . . . σπουδαιότερος of Titus), ἀναγκαῖος 1 Cor. xii. 22, 2 Cor. ix. 5, χρείας Rom. xii. 13, ἄκαρποι 1 Cor. xiv. 14.

(ii) 2 Tim. iv. 9-15, P.S. 20, 21a, Benediction 22b. Paul

writes from Nicopolis, several weeks after his note (i) summoning Titus to join him there. Autumn *c.* A.D. 56. Titus has come and gone. Timothy, now at Ephesus, is urged to come as soon as possible, in any case before winter.

> Do thy diligence to come shortly unto me : for Demas forsook me, having loved this present world, and went to Thessalonica; Crescens to Galatia, Titus to Dalmatia. Only Luke is with me. Take Mark, and bring him with thee : for he is useful to me for ministering. But Tychicus I sent to Ephesus.
>
> The cloke that I left at Troas with Carpus, bring when thou comest, and the books, especially the parchments.
>
> Alexander the coppersmith did me much evil : the Lord will render to him according to his works : of whom be thou ware also; for he greatly withstood our words.
>
> P.S. Erastus abode at Corinth : but Trophimus I left at Miletus sick. Do thy diligence to come before winter.
>
> Grace be with you.

It is clear that verses 9-12 must have been written some little time after Paul's letters to Philemon and the Colossians, in both of which Timothy is still with the Apostle, and Demas sends his greetings to the recipients. It follows that, if those letters were written at Rome – as most New Testament scholars, including the present writer, believed in 1921 – these four verses cannot belong to the same note as verses 13-15, in which Paul has been at Troas much more recently than he could have been if he were now in Rome, and Timothy needs to be told of the harm done to Paul by Alexander the coppersmith, and warned against this dangerous person.

But the belief that Colossians-Philemon were written at Rome, though still maintained by 'Conservative' scholars, is no longer held anything like so widely or so confidently as it was. In the first place, it is now much more generally recognized that the 'subscriptions' upholding this belief are of no real authority. Appended to comparatively late and inferior MSS, and so embodied in the T.R. and A.V., they are not found in the oldest and best MSS, and are rightly omitted from modern texts of the Greek New Testament and from the R.V. and the New English Bible. In the second place, the idea that all or some of the 'prison letters' (Ephesians, Philippians, Colossians and Philemon) may have been written during one, two, or even three imprisonments at Ephesus, or in that region, has been widely discussed since the publication in 1929 of Duncan's book *St. Paul's Ephesian Ministry*, and though not by any means universally accepted, is now held in one form or another by a considerable number of experts. Some reasons for believing that Philemon, much of Colossians and a letter to the Laodiceans (Col. iv. 16) now long lost, were written by St. Paul as a prisoner under house-arrest (*libera custodia*) towards the end of his Ephesian ministry, are given in an article by the present writer on 'Onesimus and Philemon' in the *Anglican Theological Review* for October 1950, and restated with additional reasons above, Chapter VII.

On this assumption there is clearly no longer any need to regard 2 Tim. iv. 9-12 and 13-15 as two different notes. These verses, with their postscript 20, 21a, stressing Paul's need for more helpers to replace those who have left him, all belong together.

Some time after sending his greeting to Philemon and the Colossians, Demas must have broken away from Paul and his company, and gone to Thessalonica, where he knew of some more lucrative employment than he could find among them (if not a 'silver mine' as in *Pilgrim's Progress*).

About Crescens we have no further information, but may surmise that Paul had sent him to Galatia (or, as ℵ has it, Gallia) on some errand connected with the great Collection (1 Cor. xvi. 1).

Titus, having joined the Apostle at Nicopolis had gone on to Dalmatia (presumably to follow up Paul's own recent visit to Illyricum (Rom. xv. 19)[1]. There was ample time for

---

[1] Cf. Tacitus, Ann, ii. 53 'honorem (consulatus) Germanicus iniit apud urbem Achaiae Nicopolim, quo venerat per Illyricam oram, viso fratre Druso in Dalmatia agente' (W. J. Woodhouse, s.v. 'Dalmatia' in Enc. Bib).

him to do this, and return to Nicopolis, while Tychicus was carrying note (ii) to Ephesus and Timothy was then coming as quickly as possible, ready to serve as joint sender of 2 Cor. i-ix, for Titus to carry when he accompanied the Macedonian delegates to Corinth (2 Cor. viii. 6, 16 ff., 23 f.).

Of all the devoted helpers who might be counted on to go anywhere and do anything they could for Paul, only Luke the beloved physician (Col. iv. 14) was with him now. Mark, the nephew of Barnabas, who was going from Ephesus (not from Rome! Col. iv. 10 f.) to Colossae, may well have accomplished that errand by now and returned to Ephesus. He has lived down his early failure (Acts xiii. 13, xv. 37 ff.), and is fully restored to Paul's confidence and favour. Like another unprofitable servant (Phmn. 11 f.) he has so ministered to Paul's needs as to make himself both profitable and a very real comfort to the Apostle. So Timothy is to pick him up and bring him along. He can be the better spared at Ephesus, and is the more needed at Nicopolis, because Paul has just sent (or is now sending, ἔπεμψα, Epistolary Aorist) Tychicus to Ephesus, perhaps with this note.

Timothy will naturally travel, as Paul himself did three months or so earlier, via Troas. He is there to call at the house of Carpus and collect the heavy winter cloak, books and parchments (i.e. notebooks, so the New English Bible), which would only have been a burden to one covering mile after mile on foot through the hot summer months after Whitsun (1 Cor. xvi. 8), but will be urgently needed when the wintry weather sets in.

In Acts xix. 23 ff., we read how Demetrius the silversmith gathered together the members of his own and allied guilds of metal-workers, and organized a protest against the interference with 'our trade'. At this meeting Alexander is put forward by the Jews to explain that he and his friends have no sort of connexion with these Christians – quite the reverse! (ἀπολογεῖσθαι) – but is shouted down by the angry crowd, to whom Jews and Christians were all one. This incident was not likely to diminish the hostility of Alexander and his party towards Paul and his friends, and they seem to have lost no time in making further trouble. Paul now in a few words

111

informs Timothy of what happened in his absence, and warns him against this dangerous man, who is sure to take any chance that offers of proving his zeal at the expense of any friend of Paul.

Not that Alexander would have confessed to any feeling so personal as a grudge. With the cold inhumanity of his kind, he would have protested that his action was dictated solely by 'principle', and was not directed against Paul and Timothy as men, but against their pernicious teaching (verse 15 λίαν γὰρ ἀντέστη τοῖς ἡμετέροις λόγοις). Any suffering inflicted on the misguided individuals who were responsible for that teaching was of course not his fault. He only did his duty. Paul understands this perfectly. Was not he too once self-betrayed by the same sophistry? But he has learned to believe in a justice which will not be deterred by any protestations of lofty motive from visiting on evil deeds their appropriate punishment. To that unerring justice he leaves this typical bigot[1], and meanwhile bids Timothy be on his guard.

Not very long before he himself left Ephesus for the last time, Paul 'sent into Macedonia two of them that ministered unto him, Timothy and Erastus,' (Acts xix. 22). The author of Acts does not say what these two were to do when they got there. Having duly recorded the fact, he leaves it hanging in the air, and passes on to other matters. Erastus is not mentioned by him again, and Timothy only as one of those who, a year later, 'had gone before' from Philippi, 'and were waiting for us at Troas' (xx. 4 f.). There is, however, no need for us to leave unanswered the question that asks itself at this point, what was the purpose of this errand? Knowing as we do from Paul's letters written before and after he left Ephesus how much that great Collection for the poor at Jerusalem was on his mind at this time (1 Cor. xvi. 1 ff., Gal. ii. 10,

---

[1] ἀποδώσει vs. 14 'will render', not ἀποδῴη 'may the Lord reward . . .', is quite certainly the true reading here. So ℵ*CD*FG, Edd., R.V. Paul is not expressing a vindictive desire that A. may get his deserts, as suggested by the Optative of T.R. and A.V., but his deep conviction, in accordance with the fundamental Christian doctrine, that God will on the Judgement Day render to each man according to his works, as foretold in Psalm lxii. 12, which he is quoting here as in Rom. ii. 6.

2 Cor. viii, ix), and remembering what he says in his defence before Felix at Caesarea, 'Now after many years I came' (to Jerusalem) 'to bring alms to my nation and offerings' (Acts xxiv. 17), we can confidently accept this as the answer to our question. In preparation for Paul's own coming to Macedonia (xix. 21), Timothy will have explained to Christians in those parts the reasons for this appeal, and done his best to win for it their whole-hearted support, before going on to Corinth, where a much more difficult task awaited him (1 Cor. xvi. 10 f.). Then Erastus will have given those Macedonian churches the benefit of his advice and help in organizing the business end of this effort. That he was quite exceptionally well qualified to do just this, is proved beyond a shadow of doubt by the fact that only a little later he was appointed by the proper authorities at Corinth to be city steward ($\acute{o}$ οἰκονόμος τῆς πόλεως) in that great commercial centre (Rom. xvi, 23). In due course, his work in Macedonia well done, he will have followed Timothy to Corinth, to render the same kind of service there. But this time, when his work for Paul was finished, he did not move on to some other place. Nor did he, like Timothy, return to Ephesus. In his postscript to the present note Paul mentions that Erastus was staying on at Corinth.

That Erastus did indeed stay on at Corinth is confirmed, and the reason for his doing so is made clear, at the end of another postscript, appended to the brief note commending to the Christian leaders at Ephesus Phoebe, who brought with her a second copy, specially made for them by the faithful Tertius, of Paul's newly completed Epistle to the Romans (i-xv). See above Chapter IX, Rom. xvi.

While Paul was writing at Corinth his Epistle to the Romans, then, the 'stewardship' of that city, which had fallen vacant, was given by those responsible for this appointment to Paul's friend Erastus.

According to the R.V. and to the New English Bible Erastus was now the 'treasurer of the city'. If this rendering of the word οἰκονόμος were correct, as most commentators assume, he must indeed have attained high office involving no small financial responsibility, and Sanday and Headlam might well suggest that he is 'presumably mentioned as the most influential member of the community' – (meaning of course the Christian community). He must have been not only, like Paul, a Roman citizen, but also a Roman magistrate, in this Roman colony.

But see further on this office, and on the life-story of this good and faithful servant, Chapter IX, Erastus and his pavement.

When Paul reminds his Corinthians that 'not many' of them were 'wise after the flesh, not many mighty, not many noble', (I Cor. i. 26), this suggests that some of them, though only a few, did have the advantage, such as it is, of belonging to the 'upper crust' of society, and could exercise the sort of influence which belongs exclusively to the 'well-born'. If one of these told those responsible for this appointment about the good work done recently by Erastus in that matter of the Collection, this may have reinforced any testimonials from his previous employers, and so helped to turn the scale in his favour.

If so, it was not the first time in the history of Greek cities that competence and devotion to duty on a comparatively small scale led to promotion to some larger sphere. Readers of Herodotus, of whom there may well have been some in higher circles at Corinth, were familiar with the story told by 'the father of history' (V. xxviii, f.) – how Miletus came to flourish again in the days of Darius, after its fortunes had sunk to a low ebb through constant factions. The Milesians call in the Parians to propose and initiate measures of reform. A small party of Parians come to Miletus, and go through its country-side, taking notes. Wherever they find a field well cultivated – and they find very few – they enter the name of its cultivator in a special list. Then they advise the Milesians to appoint the men on this list their administrators, and to do whatever they ordain.

So too in the Corinth of that first Christian century the principle that a man who has shown competence and fidelity in a limited sphere can be counted on to show the same qualities in a larger one, if he is given the chance, may well have struck those men in authority as sound common-sense –

though they had never heard it put so well as it had been a quarter of a century or so earlier by the Carpenter of Nazareth. 'He that is faithful in that which is least, is faithful also in much'. (Luke xvi. 10, cf. Mat. xxv. 21, 23).

Be that as it may, in his own line Erastus had now reached the top of the ladder, and we can be sure that he had done so on his merits. But he was not, like some who have done this, so uplifted by his success as to forget his old friends of earlier days. He sends them his greeting; and Paul, in passing on the message, mentions his promotion with a pride and affection which they will surely have shared.

Apart from the present note, the only occasion on which Paul is recorded to have been at Miletus was on his last journey to Jerusalem (Acts xx. 15). Trophimus was with him then (xx. 4), but nothing is said of his being left behind through illness or for any other reason, and he was still in Paul's company at Jerusalem (xx. 29). Even if there had been time for him to recover and join the Apostle – which seems more than doubtful – that cannot possibly be the occasion referred to here, because that was inside twenty days after Passover (xx. 6) and at least a month before Pentecos (xx. 16), whereas this was not until Pentecost (1 Cor. xvi. 8) the previous year.

On that later occasion, anxious as Paul and Trophimus the Ephesian, and others of the party, were to see their friends at Ephesus once more, he decided against putting in there (xx. 16 f.), on the ground that, if he was to reach Jerusalem by Pentecost, he must not waste precious time ($\chi\rho\text{ovo}\tau\rho\iota\beta\hat{\eta}\sigma\alpha\iota$). Instead he sent for the Ephesian elders to meet him at Miletus. This meant for them a journey by road of at least thirty five miles each way, and for him the need to wait there till they arrived. It certainly would seem a curious method of saving time, but for a fact which is sometimes overlooked in this connexion[1]. The port of Ephesus was always subject to one great natural drawback, which in the end proved its ruin. The channel between it and the sea was liable to become

---

[1]Ramsay, 'Paul the Traveller', p. 295.

choked with silt brought down by the river Cayster[1]. Strabo records (xiv, 1, 24, p. 641) that a breakwater built in the reign of Attalus II to relieve this tendency, had only aggravated it (συνέβη δὲ τοὐναντίον). The resulting congestion of traffic must have been almost at its worst when Paul sailed for Syria. For it was only a few years later (A.D. 61, 62) that Soranus, the energetic proconsul of Asia, cleared the channel and opened the harbour[2].

This explains Paul's choice of Miletus as the most convenient – or least inconvenient – port for communication with Ephesus, and makes it entirely credible that, on leaving Ephesus not before Pentecost the previous year, he went first to Miletus by road, taking Trophimus with him. But by the time they got there Trophimus fell sick and was evidently quite unfit to face the voyage. Paul was bound to miss his companionship as well as his devoted ministrations, but knew better than most men do how to accept the inevitable and make the best of things as they are. Having done all he could to arrange for Trophimus to be cared for until he was well enough to look after himself, he sailed to Troas without him.

Meanwhile, that is before this note reached him, Timothy will have returned to Ephesus. He was again in Paul's company when 2 Cor. i-ix was written (i. 1), and must therefore have received some message calling him to the Apostle's side. That message, if we are not mistaken, is now before us. Thus we may reasonably suppose that Paul got his warm cloak before that winter, and that, in writing 2 Cor. i-ix and Romans he was able to use those very books and parchments which had lain for some few months at the house of Carpus.

If the brief lines referring to Erastus and Trophimus were added as a postscript, either on the verso, or otherwise distinct from the rest of the note, this would explain their separation from it and their insertion, with the postscript to note (iii), at the end of 2 Timothy. Then last of all in verse 22

---

[1]Ramsay in H.D.B. i, p. 721 f.
[2]Tacitus, Ann. xvi. 23 'portui Ephesio aperiendo curam insumpserat.' See Furneaux's note ad loc., and Waddington, Fastes des prov. asiat. pp. 134–40, on the date of this proconsulate.

we have the two benedictions closing these two notes (iii) and (ii) in that order.

In addition to common words like μένω, ἔρχομαι, πορεύομαι, αἰών, ἀσθενέω, λόγος, πολλά, κακά etc., the following significant words and phrases are shared by this note (ii) with Colossians-Philemon, Galatians, Titus iii, 12-14 – note (i) – 2 Cor. i-ix and Romans, the nearest epistles in time, if our reconstruction is correct – σπούδασον ἐλθεῖν πρός με = Tit. iii. 12, πρὸ χειμῶνος cf. ibid. παραχειμάσαι, σπουδάζω Gal. ii. 10, ἡ χάρις μεθ᾽, ὑμῶν = Col. iv. 18, ἀντέστη Gal. ii. 11, ἡμέτερος Tit. iii. 14, Rom. xv. 4, εὔχρηστος εἰς διακονίαν Phmn. 11, 13 (εὔχρηστον . . . ἵνα ὑπὲρ σοῦ μοι διακονῇ), Col. iv. 18 διακονίαν, μάλιστα Phmn. 16, Gal. vi. 10, ἐγκαταλείπω 2 Cor. iv. 9, λίαν (cf. ὑπερλίαν 2 Cor. xi. 5, xii. 12), ἀποστέλλω 2 Cor. xii. 17, ἐνδείκνυμι 2 Cor. viii. 24, ἀποδώσει αὐτῷ ὁ κύριος κατὰ τὰ ἔργα αὐτοῦ = Ps. lxii. 12, cit. also Rom. ii. 6.

(iii)

PAUL'S LAST LETTER

2 Tim. i. 16-18, iii. 10, 11, iv. 1, 2a, 5b-8, 16-19, 21b, 22a. Written at Rome c. A.D. 62 on the eve, or perhaps within hours, of his martyrdom, to find Timothy at Ephesus on his arrival there from Philippi.

The brief addresses, perhaps identical, of this letter and of note (ii) appear to have been expanded in i. 1 f. to match the fuller and more formal addresses of the letters to churches. They may well have run simply 'Paul to Timothy greeting' (χαίρειν) – like countless other purely private notes and letters.

The Lord grant mercy unto the house of Onesiphorus : for he oft refreshed me, and was not ashamed of my chain; but, when he was in Rome, he sought me diligently, and found me (the Lord grant unto him to find mercy of the Lord in that day); and in how many things he ministered at Ephesus, thou knowest very well.

But thou didst follow my teaching, conduct, purpose, faith, long-suffering, love, patience, persecutions, sufferings; what things befell me at Antioch, at Iconium, at Lystra; what

117

persecutions I endured: and out of them all the Lord delivered me.

I charge thee in the sight of God, and of Christ Jesus, who shall judge the quick and the dead, and by his appearing and his kingdom; preach the word; be instant in season, out of season . . .

Do the work of an evangelist, fulfil thy ministry.

For I am already being offered, and the time of my departure is come. I have fought the good fight, I have finished the course, I have kept the faith : henceforth there is laid up for me the crown of righteousness, which the Lord, the righteous judge, shall give me in that day : and not only to me, but also to all them that have loved his appearing.

At my first defence no one took my part, but all forsook me : may it not be laid to their account. But the Lord stood by me, and strengthened me; that through me the message might be fully proclaimed, and that all the Gentiles might hear : and I was delivered out of the mouth of the lion. The Lord will deliver me from every evil work, and will save me unto his heavenly kingdom : to whom be the glory for ever and ever. Amen.

Salute Prisca and Aquila, and the house of Onesiphorus. Eubulus saluteth thee, and Pudens, and Linus, and Claudia, and all the brethren.

The Lord be with thy spirit.

The letter falls into five parts, followed by a brief postscript and benediction.

 I Onesiphorus and his labour of love, i, 16-18.

 II Timothy's own companionship over a longer period, iii, 10 f.

 III A last charge laid on Timothy to carry on the great work of preaching the Gospel, iv. 1, 2a, 5b.

 IV For Paul's own life-work is finished, and the time of his departure from this world has come, iv. 6-8.

 V The preliminary hearing of his case before Caesar has left Paul in no doubt what the verdict will be. He awaits the inevitable end with unshaken confidence in his divine Deliverer, iv. 16-18.

I

The letter begins with a grateful reference to services rendered, in Timothy's absence, by a friend from Ephesus, who had made it his business to seek out the prisoner of Tigellinus (Tac. Ann. xiv, 51) – not the easiest task in the world, nor the safest – and had found him in that closer confinement, to which he must have been transferred during or before his trial, from the hired lodging of Acts xxviii. 30.

There is a great story behind Paul's brief but suggestive record of that search through Rome. We seem to catch glimpses of one purposeful face in a drifting crowd, and follow with quickening interest this stranger from far coasts of the Aegean, as he threads the maze of unfamiliar streets, knocking at many doors, following up every clue, warned of the risks he is taking but not to be turned from his quest; till in some obscure prison-house a known voice greets him, and he discovers Paul chained to a Roman soldier.

Having once found the way, Onesiphorus is not content with a single visit, but true to his name, proves unwearied in his ministrations. Others have flinched from the menace and ignominy of that chain: but this visitor counts it the supreme privilege of his life to share with such a criminal the reproach of the Cross. One series of turnings in the vast labyrinth he comes to know as if it were his own Ephesus.

We can partly divine what these visits must have meant to one whose bodily powers, spent and broken by much privation, were in urgent need of such material comforts as Onesiphorus would not fail to bring. Still more as tokens of that love which 'never faileth', must they have refreshed a spirit jaded by suspense, disappointed and saddened by recent experience of cynical injustice and craven disloyalty.

For in those days his Roman citizenship had proved to be a worthless thing, and Roman justice a mockery. When he was awaiting his trial, some members of the church at Rome, so far from even trying to help him, had been active in making of the Gospel itself a tool to damage his case. In that he had contrived to find a reason for rejoicing[1], as Timothy, who was

---

[1] Phil. i. 15, 17 f.

with him at that time, will doubtless remember. Nor was that all. Some, who had seemed to favour his cause, had withdrawn their support in these last critical days. Alarmed by ominous signs of coming storm, they had openly disclaimed any sympathy with him and his aims, proving only too conclusively that in their minds, after all, their own interests came first, not 'the things of Jesus Christ'[1]. So Paul was left almost if not quite alone. For he had felt it right to send some others, besides Timothy, on errands of vital importance, setting the requirements of the kingdom, as always, before his own necessities, e.g. Epaphroditus[2] and Luke[3]. Lonely and tired and ill, he would not have been human if those desertions had not cut him to the quick. Yet of all this he now says not a word, and only speaks with passionate gratitude of the relief brought by this faithful friend.

But Onesiphorus has paid his last visit. Paul does not say what has become of him. For others' sakes, as well as his own, the prisoner must be careful what he writes. Some things must always be left for a trusty messenger to tell by word of mouth. That he had taken many and great risks for Paul, and for the work of Christ, is certain. He who so risks his life, has given it, whether or not he receive it again. The impression conveyed to most readers is that Onesiphorus had ventured into this dangerous quarter once too often, and paid, or seemed likely to pay, the penalty with his life. But see above p. 51 f. on the possible identity of Onesiphorus with Onesimus.

Paul's prayer for him is that in the Hereafter he may be repaid in his own coin by One, whose promise stands, 'Blessed are the merciful, for they shall obtain mercy'. As he had persevered till he found Paul in this dark cell, so in that bright Day when he reaches the goal of his life's quest, may he find a still truer Friend, and better welcome, awaiting him There. Meanwhile in one household at Ephesus they may be needing that same mercy to comfort them, when they hear the news that will accompany this letter. He prays that they may find it; and sends them such an account of those last weeks at Rome, as would at least mingle a just pride with

---

[1]Phil. ii. 21.   [2]Phil. x. 25.   [3]See below, p.126.

their sorrow. So he discharges this debt of gratitude as best he can – pays an immortal tribute to the memory of his friend, rescues his name from oblivion, and links it for ever with his own, as one of those who held not their lives of any account, so that they might accomplish the ministry which they received from the Lord Jesus (Acts xx. 24).

That Onesiphorus should have proved himself worthy of such a tribute would be no surprise to those who had known the man long and well enough to recognize his real character. It was like him, they would say, recalling one instance after another of his thoughtful self-effacing ministry. There was one time in particular, five to seven years earlier, when he and Paul and Timothy were all in Ephesus together. Doubtless Timothy had every reason to realize then, and to remember now, how well this true disciple had learned the lesson taught in those 'words of the Lord Jesus' – 'It is more blessed to give than to receive' (Acts xx. 35).

A comparison of this passage with that in which Paul tells the Philippians (ii. 25 ff.) of similar services rendered, and risks taken, by Epaphroditus, leaves no room for doubt that he who wrote the one, wrote also the other, and after no long interval. Each helps us to understand how it was that so many were willing to put their lives in jeopardy for his sake.

II

But Paul was not one to keep all his gratitude for the dead, and forget what he owed to the living friend, whose services and comradeship reached back over a still longer period.

For himself the thought of what is coming has no terrors. For Love and Faith have transfigured Death, and banished Fear. But he realizes none the less what the news of his death must mean to Timothy. With infinite care and delicacy he chooses his words to break the shock of those tidings, and comfort the sad heart of his friend. First he will rob inevitable grief at least of its sting, by meeting beforehand all bitter thoughts of vain regret or needless self-reproach, that Timothy was not in his place by Paul's side at the last. He will set What-has-been to silence What-might-have-been. Then he will show him the brighter side of this sorrow.

Nothing that any one else may have done, and nothing that has happened, or can happen now, will ever be able to eclipse the unwavering devotion of this man after Paul's own heart, this kindred spirit (ἰσόψυχον, Phil. ii. 20), who has followed like his faithful shadow over more miles than either of them could count. Long before ever they set foot in Ephesus as heralds of the Gospel, Timothy had responded with youthful enthusiasm to Paul's invitation, and had left all, to join him on what was then already a perilous mission. He knows, none better, what happened to Paul before that, at Antioch, at Iconium, and at Lystra. No need to write out the much longer list of places where they two together have since then carried their lives in their hands, as they flung in the face of an unbelieving world the eternal challenge of the Cross. Uphill and down, through storm and sunshine, leaving the old home very far behind, they have walked side by side, learning to know and understand each other, as only they can, who have seen one another in many different lights and changing moods, and under very varied circumstances. In the fierce furnace of tribulation, and in the crucible of pain, they have proved each the other's fidelity, and have found it pure gold.

It does not seem too much to say that Timothy must indeed have 'followed' Paul's teaching, alike in its detail and in its large outlines, as no other ever did or ever will. For when Paul was writing his early letters to the Thessalonians, as in his varied correspondence with the Corinthian Church, Timothy was there by his side. When he was a prisoner at Ephesus, Timothy was with him as he wove the rich fabric of his charge to the church at Colossae, and revealed in his note to Philemon more of the real Paul than any but an intimate might see. When he dictated at Corinth his master-piece to the Romans, Timothy was there while Tertius wrote. Last of all in Rome, only a little while ago, when he opened his heart to those loyal friends at Philippi, Timothy was there, not as an absolutely silent and impassive bystander, but venturing perhaps now and then to offer a suggestion. In every Epistle, except Galatians and the pseudonymous Ephesians, he is named either as a trusted colleague or as joint-sender along with Paul; and this can hardly have been a mere idle compliment.

He knew therefore the actual circumstances under which each of these immortal letters was written. He could recall the very look, tone, and gesture with which many of those thoughts were first uttered, that have changed so many lives. There would be other letters too, doubtless, known to Timothy, but lost to us, (e.g. to the Laodiceans, Col. iv. 16).

He has had unique opportunities of following not only the written, but also the spoken words of the Apostle – sermons on great occasions, discussions in school and synagogue, fierce debates, conversations in street or market or upper room – personal applications of one divine remedy to the infinite variety of human need.

Meanwhile his youth has hardened into manhood, and the disciple (or Chela, as they might say in India), has become the beloved and trusty comrade. Sharing the vision of a Kingdom, they have shared also the travail which makes that Kingdom come. They have learned to be silent together without embarrassment, or speak without reserve, as men may, who have passed through deep waters together. And this old fisher of men might have repeated what that other old fisherman, in Theocritus, says to his mate, as they lie in their hut by the sea, wakeful through the long, dark hour before down:

$$\dot{\omega}_S \; \kappa a i \; \tau \grave{a} \nu \; \mathring{a}\gamma \rho a \nu \; \tau \hat{\omega}\nu \epsilon i \rho a \tau a \; \pi \acute{a} \nu \tau a \; \mu \epsilon \rho i \zeta \epsilon \nu^1$$

So it has come to pass that Timothy has been initiated into the inner secrets of Paul's mind, has marked the drift of his great arguments and the connexion between diverse elements in his teaching – has entered into his aims and ideals, his hopes and fears, his dreams and disappointments, and shared with him the ventures of that faith which stakes all on the present power, and final victory, of 'things not seen'. He has come very near to the great heart of Paul, has caught the glow of its passion, felt the throb of its desire, and marvelled at the inexhaustible reserves of its calm fortitude.

He knows too, as hardly another, what it has all cost –

---

[1] Idyll xxi. 31: 'Be partner of my dreams, as of my fishing' – A. C. Benson, *Upton Letters*, p. 282.

amid what difficulties, in what sheer physical weakness, weariness and pain, and in the teeth of what relentless opposition, open and underhand, Paul has carried out his life-purpose through the years. It was a hunted man, with a price set on his head, as well as a sick man, tortured and hampered by some incurable complaint, who built up that mighty edifice, to withstand the shocks of time, and become one of the permanent factors shaping the thoughts and moulding the destinies of men. Yes, Timothy knows, though he cannot understand, the hatred which has dogged the steps of his friend – by what awful vows men with pious phrases on their lips have bound themselves to kill him – and by how very little they have failed. But one thing more he knows, that hitherto the Unseen Deliverer has brought him safely through all.

Therefore he has the right to share Paul's confidence that in this direst assault of evil powers the same Divine Helper will stand by him to the end. This does not mean that Paul is blind to the desperate nature, humanly speaking, of his present situation. When he wrote to the Philippians, there still seemed quite a good hope of his being set free to revisit his charches, and continue his work on earth. But now that is all over, and there is not the remotest chance of his escaping alive from the hands of his enemies.

When this letter reaches Ephesus, Timothy will not lack friends there who, sharing his grief, will do what sincere sympathy can to comfort him. But Paul knows him well enought to foresee that he will need more than sympathy, however true and deep. For the rest of his life he will have to do without Paul's help and guidance, on which he has so long been accustomed to lean and rely. He must learn to stand on his own feet and make his own decisions. He will also be in constant need of some strong encouragement and stimulus, to overcome his natural timidity (1 Cor. xvi. 10). So now –

III

the Apostle lays on Timothy the last solemn charge, in the witnessing presence of mighty Invisible Powers, binding him to his duty by vows more strait than ever Arthur laid upon his knights. Come what may, he is to herald the Word. Let his message ring out inevitable as the Day of Judgement, and his preaching catch from his theme some of its tremendous urgency. Keep close at the appointed task (ἐπίστηθι), as one whose Taskmaster is close at hand (ἐφέστηκεν, cf. 1 Thess. v. 2 f. ἐπίσταται). This he must do, not waiting for the convenient season, like some excellent persons and brilliant preachers (1 Cor. xvi. 12 ὅταν εὐκαιρήσῃ), but sowing the good seed in all weathers and beside all waters. 'In season', yes, watching always for the best opportunity, missing no heaven-sent chance, buying up the right moment, though it cost all he has. But also, 'out of season' – daring the apparently hopeless venture, holding on when all seems lost, preaching to deaf ears, knocking still at fast-bolted doors, finding in opposition and peril only an added incentive to go forward (1 Cor. xvi. 8 f.). Timothy is to do the work not of an ecclesiastic, (honorurable and necessary as later experience may prove such service to be), but of an evangelist. His to take up the torch and wave it; to carry the light of a great Hope into the dark places of sorrow, sin, and despair; and so labouring to fill up his cup of human service.

IV

For Paul's own cup is full to the brim, nay is already being poured out (see p. 92). At last he has received the summons so long and eagerly awaited. For him the midnight is past. He stands watching the day break. His hour of destiny has come. The anchor is weighed, the vessel ready. A wind from heaven is filling her sails. And the voyager is ready too. It is high time for him to put out to sea. There will be no shipwreck this time!

So in Paul's spirit broods the deep content of one who has played his part like a man in the great game of life. He has run his race. He has kept the faith, not like some zealous custodian of traditions received, at second-hand, from a mightier Past, but as a pioneer guards the gate of a land he helped to discover; as a seeker stands for the Truth revealed to his eyes by no mortal's showing, but by a light from heaven.

All that remains for him now is to go and receive the

125

victor's crown, laid up in store for him in some safe treasure-house of the great Unseen. This a Judge more just than Caesar will give him on that Day whose promised coming is the refrain of Paul's triumph-song. But not Paul only – there would be no joy for him in any reward which he could not look forward to sharing with others – all who have loved the Lord's appearing, shall have their part in the glory of that marvellous dawn.

V

Having read so far Timothy will naturally be eager to learn how Paul knows that his end is so near, in other words, exactly what happened at that long delayed hearing of his case before Caesar, for which a date had at last been fixed when he sent Timothy to Philippi with the news (Phil. ii. 19, 23).

At the time of writing, the preliminary hearing (*prima actio*) is over, and the final hearing is due to take place almost immediately. Caesar will then pronounce his sentence, from which there can be no appeal.

At that 'first defence' no man took his part. Of the devoted little company, any one of whom would have stood by him to the death, not one is now in Rome. Onesiphorus has paid, or seems likely to pay, with his life for his devotion. Epaphroditus is back at Philippi, whither Paul had 'counted it necessary' to send him. If Luke were now in Rome, he would never have left Paul in the lurch. Wherever he may be, we can be sure Paul had counted it necessary in his case too. Timothy will have gone on for the same reason from Philippi to Ephesus, where this letter will find him. The good friends greeted in Romans xvi are not in Rome but at Ephesus, as we have seen (above, p. 88). Of the mixed company with which he had been in touch lately, some, as Timothy knows, have preached Christ of envy and strife, thinking to stir up trouble for Paul, and it looks now as if their activities may not have been entirely without effect. Others are compara-tively new friends, of whose sincerity and personal goodwill he has no doubt, but whom he did not expect to go with him into the lion's den. They would only have got themselves into trouble, without really helping him. He does not blame them, and hopes no one else will. But among those who knew the Apostle and had seemed friendly towards him, there may well have been some who might have said or done something to help him in his dire predicament. In Rome, as at Corinth, there may have been just a few Christians whose birth and social status gave them an influence far beyond that enjoyed by most of their fellow-members[1]. But not one of them had said a word, or lifted a finger, on his behalf. He prays that this may not be held against them at the great Assize.

So at long last Paul has stood before Caesar, alone yet not alone. One who has never yet failed him, and never will, stood by his side. The strength that is made perfect in weakness was granted him in fullest measure just when he needed it most. This is one of those echoes from Philippians which make it certain that that letter was written not long before this his last[2]. There nothing is impossible to Paul 'in him that strengtheneth me' (ἐν τῷ ἐνδυναμοῦντί με Phil. iv. 13). Here the Lord has given him strength (ὁ κύριος . . . ἐνεδυνάμωσέν με) to achieve the impossible by making of that dread hour the climax of his career as a herald of the Gospel – an opportunity to blow his Lord's trumpet for the last time in the one place where, if anywhere on earth, he could say (giving Timothy credit for enough sense not to take his words too literally), 'that all the nations might hear'.

He has come through that 'first' ordeal not only alive, having been saved, in the words of the Psalmist (xxii. 22), 'from the mouth of the lion', but with flying colours. Now with dauntless courage and triumphant faith he awaits the imminent second hearing and Caesar's verdict. Not that he is under any illusion as to what that verdict will be. Himself no mean judge of character, he has come face to face with a Nero freed from the restraining influence of Burrus and Seneca, and now egged on by Tigellinus and Poppaea to gave his basest impulses the rein. This is the end, and Paul knows it. Yet even so he is safe. For the same divine Helper, who has

---

[1]See Lightfoot, *S. Clement of Rome*, I, p. 29 ff., 1898.
[2]See above, p. 92f.

brought him safely through so many and great dangers, will deliver him from every evil work, and bring him safely through the very jaws of death into His heavenly kingdom.

This noble passage fitly ends with the Doxology. There is indeed nothing more to be said. A last greeting to Paul's chief friends at Ephesus, Prisca and Aquila, who risked their lives for him long ago (Rom. xvi. 3 f.), and would do it again, if occasion offered; and the family of Onesiphorus. Then greetings to Timothy from four members of the Roman Church by name, and from the brethren generally. The letter closes with the simple benediction.

Of this last message Bengel's golden phrase tells the whole truth, and nothing but the truth:

'Testamentum Pauli et cygnea cantio est haec epistula'[1]

To these three notes the oracular remark of Erasmus may be applied, without a trace of that irony which seems to lurk in the words, so often as they are quoted with reference to these Epistles as a whole:

'Non est cujusvis hominis Paulinum pectus effingere'.[2]

There is a saying attributed to Averrhoes, the Arab philosopher:

'Bonum est cribrare modium sabuli ut quis inveniat unam margaritam'.[3]

It has been necessary for us to sift many bushels of the dryest sand that ever drifted – collecting Particles, Prepositions, *Hapex Legomena*, passing these through index after index as through a sieve – calculating percentages, poring over diagrams, and striving to wrest from arid pages of statistics their lost secret. Now at the end, if our argument holds, we find not one pearl only, but three, and see them restored, each to its own place on the shining thread of Paul's lifestory.

---

[1]'This letter is Paul's testament and swan-song'.
[2]'Not every man can feign the heart of Paul.'
[3]'It is good to sift a measure of sand, and find one pearl' – E. C. Gardner, *Dante's Ten Heavens*, p. 3.

32 Words found in the Pastorals, but not elsewhere in the N.T., nor in
Goodspeed's *Indices (Patristicus et Apologeticus)*. Sixty one ● not in LXX.
Three [ ] in the Genuine Notes.

, ● ἀδηλότης i. Protag., Polyb., Philo, Cornelius (i A.D.), Plut. (II times in
D.Wyttenbach, *Plutarchi Index Graecitatis*, Oxon.1830), Dio Chrys. 66 (xvi) 8.

● αἱρετικός ii. Ps.Plat., *Def.* = 'able to choose', Hierocl. Stoic. (i/ii A.D.)= 'due
to choice', Aelian, N.A. 6.59 (in general sense), Paulus Alex. Q.2 (Astrol.iv A.D.)

● αἰσχροκερδής V. Eurip., Hdt., Plat., Aristot., ..Philo, Plut., Vett.Valens 74².
[ἀκαίρως] ii. Lxx Sir. xxiv (xxxi)4, Aeschyl., Hippocr.,Philo,Joseph., Epict., Dio Chrys., Galen.
ἀκατάγνωστος iii. Lxx 2 Macc.iv.47, Rhet.Gr.I 597, Inscr.C.I.G. 1971.b.5 A.D.165.

● ἄμαχος V. = 'no brawler', since Xenophon, Jos. Ant.XV.5.1, Plut. 2,667D ἄμαχος
γὰρ ἡ φιλοφροσύνη, Epigr.Gr. 387,6, Inscr. of Cos '91, 325,9.D. (Paton&Hicks).
(= 'unconquerable' or 'Irresistible' Dio Chrys. 3 (II) 5, Plut. Camill.xxxix.150,
Appian, Hisp.97 etc, and in the Classics).

● ἀνδραποδιστής i. since Aristoph., Plato, Xen, Demosth, Polyb, Philo, Spec.Leg. IV(6)13,
Dio Chrys. 52 (LXIX)9, Plut. quaest. Conviv.II.vii, Zenob.V.36, Artemid.Dald,
Onirocrit. (ed. Hercherus, 1864) p.210,12, Lucian,Dial.Deor.4,1,209 etc.

● ἀνεπαίσχυντος ii.Joseph. Ant.XVII.7.1, Agapetus,De Offic.boni princ.57.p.174.

● ἀντιξμετίθεμαι ii. Philo, Spec.Leg. IV (4)103, Apollonius Dysc. Synt.iii.170 bis,
Longinus 17.1 iii A.D. (Active -ημι = 'retaliate upon' Diod. Sic.34.12 i.B.C).

● ἀντίθεσις i. Plato, Aristot., Hermog. progymn.ii et passim ii A.D., Philo, Ebr.187,
Plut., de primo frig.xvii bis, Apollon.Dysc., Synt.iii.184, Lucian,Dial.Mort.10,10
(374), Demosth. Enc.8 (496), Galen, De Temp. 4,10 et passim.

● ἀντίλυτρον i. Zenob. Cent.II.48, Polyaen. Exc.52.7, (Orph.Lith.593 =
antidote, remedy)

● ἀπόβλητος i. Since Homer, Philo, Spec.Leg.II.169, Plut.I 821 A, Dio Chrys.4(IV)93,
Apollon.Dysc., Synt.ii.126, Lucian, Timon 37 (149), Tox.37 (545),DeMerc.Con.
27 (686), Philops. 29 (56).
ἀποθησαυρίζω i. Lxx Sir. 3,4, Diod.Sic.5,40, Joseph., B.J.VII.5.2, 8.4,
Epict.II.xvii.50, Artemid I.73 p.66,22, Vett.Val.16²¹, 18⁷, Aelian,N.A.III.10,
XIV.18, Lucian, Alex. 23 (231).

● ἄρτιος ii. since Homer, Diod. Sic. 3.33, Epict.,I.xviii.3, II.xvi.2, Plut.,
Numa 14, Symp.IX.vi, M.Aurel.Anton. I.16.31, Theon.Smyrn. (ed. Hiller, Lips.
1878),p.23.8, 24.5, Hephaestio (M.Corsbruch, Lips.1906),p.21.24, 22.2,
Nichomachus Gerasenus (R.Hoche, Lips. 1866) I.7.2,5, Lucian.De Sacr.6.

● ἄσπονδος ii. since Aeschyl., Polyb., Philo, de Sacrif. (4) 7, (5) 32,Virt. 131,Joseph.,
Ant.IV.8.24,XV.5.3, Dio Chrys. 57 (LXXIV)3, Plut., Pericl.xxx, Polyaenus,
(Woelfflin, Lips.1887) VIII.95,65, Lucian, Alex.25 (235), Appian, Sam. 4,2,
Galen (Helmreich, 1907)II p. 195, 15.

● αὐθέντης i. Philod.rhet.II p.133.14 (i B.C), BGU 1208.307 (i B.C.),
Ptolem. apotel.3.14.10, Mich.Glycas 270,10 (I.Bekker, 1836)αἱ γυναῖκες
αὐθεντοῦσι τῶν ἀνδρῶν.

● αὐτοκατάκριτος iii. Philo II 652 (Fragm.in John of Damascus ,ed.Mangey II 65
cf. *Fragmenta Philonis* ed.J.Reader Harris, Cambridge,1886,
Pseudo-Justin, *Ep.ad Zenam et Serenam* 17 (ed.J.C.T.Otto, III.1.p.34).

ρ ἀφθορία ἴ. Lxx Haggai ii.17, one MS. A, reads ἀφορία for ἀφορία or ἀπορία (ΟΙϑϑἧ = blight, of crops). In Tit.ii.7 ἀ. = 'uncorruptness' AV,RV, 'integrity' NEB. Cf. Themistius Soph. in Aristotelis Physica paraphrasis, ed. H.Schenkl, Berlin, 1900, 82.21 (iv A.D).
ἄφθορος Lxx Esther ii.2, Justin D. 100.5, Ap.15.6, Diod.Sic.4.7.3 (i B.C), Artemid.Dald., Onirocrit.Libri V ed. R.Hercherus, Lips.1864, V 95 = p.275, Dio Chrys. 11 (XV) 49, Plut. de def. orac. xix., Appian,B.C.II 22, Galen 8.421, 424.14, Phalaris, ep.70 (vi B.C.), BGU 1106.11, 110.7, ZF (=Die Graeci Zauberpapyri, K.Preisendanz, Papyri Graeci Magicae, 1928,1931) 5.376, 7.554.

● ἀφιλάγαθος ii.   (Φιλάγαθος Dio Chrys. 34(L)3, Plut. I 37E, I 140c, Vet.Val.104, ἀφιλόκαλος Plut., I 672E, Galen 5.39, ἀφιλόσοφος Justin 7, App.3:11(kua, ἀφιλοξενία I Clem. 35.5.

  βαθμός i. Lxx 4.Ki.xx.9 sq. = degree on the dial, Sir.vi.36 β.θυρῶν, doorstep or threshold. II metaph. = step or degree in rank, Artem.II 42, οἱ β.Κλίμακος προκοπήν σημαίνουσι, Procopius Caes.Historicus, Historia Arcana 24(vi A.D.) Lydus, Mag.2.8 (vi A.D), =rank Lucian, Amores 53 (456), simply = degree Joseph.,B.J.IV 3 10, Dio Chrys. 24 (xliv6 in a genealogy, two 'steps' farther back than ones grandfather, Philo, aet. mund.58, Appian, Pun.130, Hermetica (W.Scott, 13.9). Hadrian Imp. Sententiae (Estienne, Thes. Gr. Ling. xii. 2.490f. The Emperor tells a soldier who wants to join the Praetorian Guard, to prove his mettle first in service with the militia, ἐν τῇ πολιτικῇ στρατεία. καὶ ἐὰν καλὸς στρατιώτης γένῃ, τρίτῳ βαθμῷ δυνήσῃ εἰς πραιτώριον μεταβῆναι. cf. I Tim.III. 13 οἱ γὰρ καλῶς διακονήσαντες βαθμὸν ἑαυτοῖς καλόν περιποιοῦνται.

● γάγγραινα ii. Hippocr. Mochl. 33 (a section of dubious authenticity,— so H.Stuart Jones told me long ago). Diosc.1.61, Soranus,Gyn.II.61, Galen, de tumor.8 etc.,— all = 'gangrene' as a technical medical term. Figuratively Plut., II 65b = de adulat.et amic. xxvi.

● γενεαλογία v. Isocr., Plato, Polyb. γεν. καὶ μῦθοι Philo, de cong. erud(8)44, Joseph. Ant. XI 3 10, c. Apion I 4, Plut. Numa XVIII (72), Soranus (Ideler) I p.52.

● γραώδης i. Chrysipp. Stoic. II 255 (III B.C), comp. -ἑστερος Galen, 5.315, μυθάριον γραώδες Cleomedes 2.1, γραωδ. μυθολογία Strabo I.23.

  γυμνασία i. Lxx 4 Macc.xi.20, Plato, Polyb, Strabo III.2.7, Dio Chrys. 79 (xxviii) 3, Epict., I 7 n,18, 8.7, 27.6, III 23.2, Plut. II 69B, 646A, 1022c, SIG 1075.19 (ii A.D).
● γυναικάριον ii. Diocles Comicus I, Epict., Ench.7, M.Anton. V.11.

● διαπαρατριβή i.   (παρατριβή Polyb.2.36.5, Athenaeus Gram. 14.626 e (ii/iii A.D.), Athenag. διατριβαί Dio Chrys.8 (ix)2, Lucian,Adv.Indoct.3 διαπαρατηθέομαι Lxx 2 Ki.3.30.
● διδακτικός iv. Philod.rhet.p. 22¹⁰ (i B.C) Philo, Congr.7 (35), Praem. 4.(27).
● ἑδραίωμα i. Letter of the churches of Lyons and Vienne (A.D.178, Euseb.H.E.V.I.17).
  ἔκδηλος ii. Lxx 3 Macc.iii.19, vi.5, Homer, Ep.Arist.85 (ii B.C), Philo, Leg.Alleg. II.8.30, Plut. I 220 B, II 666 F,DioChrys.13 (VII)142,8(IX)2,53 (LXX)7, 80 (xxx)5, Nichomachus Ger. (R.Hoche, Lips.1866)I.5.2, II.20.3, II.22.3. Vett.Val 92ᵘ.
● ἐκζήτησις i   (ἐκζητέω Lxx   I Clem 35.5 etc. Hermas Vis. 3:3.15 etc. Bar. 1014 etc., Did.4.12, Ζήτησις Justin, Melito,Dio Chr.76(xxvii)4)
  ἔλεγμός ii. Only in Lxx, various meanings, = reproof Sir.21⁶, 35 (32)17, ἐπανόρθωσις ii. Lxx I Es. 8⁵², I Macc.xiv.34, Aristot. Eth.Nic.IX ii.9, Ep.Arist. 130.283. Polyb.1.66.12, Philo, Leg.Alleg. I (3)85, Aelia (3)13 Dio Chr. 21(xxvii)9, 14.(xxxi) 66, Epict.III.24⁵, Plut.,I 790f,II 1016 C, Galen, de Temp.(Helmreich)2672.
  ἐπαρκέω i. Lxx I Macc.viii 26, xi.35, Homer, Polyb.1.51.10, Joseph, Ant XV 96, Dio Chr. 13 (VII) 61, 21 (xxxviii) 33, Epict.,II.26.8,Plut.I798,II 1118 c,Lucian,Nigr.26.
● ἐπιΔααθόω II. GDI.5029.9 (Hieropytna ii.B.C), Themistius, Or.7 p.119 A- (iv A.D), Syrianus, in Metaph.167.11 (V. A.D).

- ἐπιστομίζω iii. Aristoph. *Equ.* 845, Plato, *Philo, de pot.insid.* (8) 23, Joseph., *Ant.* XVII 101, Plut., I 192 E, I 592 B, etc. Lucian, *pro imag.* 10 (490), *calum. ne tem.cred.* 2 (142).
- εὐμετάδοτος I. M.Anton., I 44, VI 48 I, Vett.Val. 7[13] 11[2] 12[6] 42[3] 46[8.24] 28[8] 82[4] Vit.Aesopi (ed. Eberhard, 1872) I c.26, p. 289.1, *Hermias in Phaedr.* p.94 (v A.D.).
- θεόπνευστος ii. Pseudo-Phocyl. 129 (Anthol.lyr.gr. I[2], ed.E.Diehl, 1936), Plut., I 904 F, Vett.Val. 330[19], Or. Sib. 5 308. 406.
- ἱεροπρεπής iii. LXX 4 Macc. ix.25, xi.20, Philo, *Leg. Alleg.* III (72) 204, etc. Joseph., *Ant.* XI 85, Plut., II.11 c., Zenob. IV.29, Lucian *de sacr.* (13) 537.
- καλοδιδάσκαλος iii. (κακοδιδασκαλέω 2 Clem. X.5,) Sextus Emp. *adv. Math.* 2.42 (ed. H.Mutschmann, Lips. 1912–) ii. A.D, –ία Ign. *Phil.* ii.1, *Eph.* xvi.2 [Lft.]).
- καταστολή i. LXX Is. lxi.3, Hippocr. *Decent.* 5.8, Ep.Arist. 284[2], Joseph., B.J. II 84, Epict., II 10 15, 21 11, Plut., I 154 c., Soranus, *Gyn.* I 86.
- καταστρηνιάω i.
- καυστηριάζομαι i. (So ℵ Ti, WH, Nestle 1 Tim. iv.2) In this form the only known parallels are Leontios 40, p.79.9 vi A.D., and perhaps BGU 952.4 i/ii A.D., and much less probably in a var.lect. of Strabo 5.1.9 ed. J. Kramer, 1844, where A.Meinecke, Lips. 1921 omits the σ. Souter and von Soden follow the majority of MSS in reading κεκαυτηριασμένων 1 Tim. iv.2. With this cf. Hippiatr. 1.28. Schol. in Lucian (ed. H. Rabe, Lips.1906) 137[2] κεκαυτηριασμένος κυρίως ὁ μὴ ἔχων ὑγιῆ τὴν συνείδησιν.
  Pseudo-Ign. *ad Antioch.* 11 (latter half of iv A.D. Lft.)
- κενοφωνία iv. Diosc. *de Mat.Med. praef.* 2, Porphyry *adv Christ.* 58.15 (ed. Harnack, 19 6) iii A.D., Justinian, *Impr.Novellae* 146.1.2 (R.Schoel and W.Kroll, Berlin, 1905) vi A.D.
- κνήθω ii. Aristot., Strato Epigr. (Anth.Pal. ed. H. Stadtmüller, Lips. 1894–1906) 12.258.8 (ii A.D.), Apollonius Dysc., *Synt.* iii 160 (ed.R.Schneider and G.Uhlig, Lips. 1878–1910) ii A.D., Herodian, 43,34. (Gramm. Gr., ed. G. Dindorf, Lips. 1823) ii A.D. Moeris κνῆν Ἀττικοί, κνήθειν Ἕλληνες (Lex. Att. ed. G.Koch, Lips. 1830, p. 234) ii A.D., Clem. Alex., *Strom.* I.iii.22 (iii A.D.). Cf. Lucian, *de Salt.* (13) 266 τὸ ὅμοιον πεπονθὼς τοῖς τὰ ὦτα πτερῷ κνωμένοις. Plut., II 167 B Μουσικήν φησι, ν ὁ Πλάτων,... εὐρυθμίας δημιουργόν, ἀνθρώποις ὑπὸ θεῶν οὐ τρυφῆς ἕνεκα καὶ κνήσεως ὤτων δοθῆναι (Plat., *Rep.* III E).
- κοινωνικός i. Aristot., Polyb., 2.44.1, Philo, *Migr. Abr.* (28) 156 etc. Epict., 123 1, II 10 4, etc, Plut., II 167 B, Artemid. IV 56, Galen, *Temp.* I xii.13, Vett.Valens 104[15] 198[16] 339[17], M.Antonin., V.6.6, Ptolem., *Tetr.* 69 (ii A.D.).
- λογομαχέω ii. Eustath., *opusc.* p. 47, 96 (xii A.D.).
- λογομαχία i. Varro, who died 27 B.C., used this word as title of a Menippean Satire, according to Nonius Marcellus, the 4th-century grammarian, p.268 L. Conon, *narrat.* 38, (i B.C./i A.D.) is quoted by Photius, *bibl. cod.* 186, as using this word. Porphyry is quoted as using it by Euseb. *praep. ev.* 14.10,2 . See too Cat. cod. astr. VII 1 p.167. Also Porphyr. *ad* Hor. *Sat.* 2.4. Cf. Conon historicus in Fragmente der griechischen Historiker, ed. F. Jacoby, Berlin 1923– , 1. p.190.
- μάμμη ii. (1. = child's word for Mother, Pherecrates V B.C., Menander Com. iv/iii B.C.). 2. = grandmother LXX 4 Macc. xvi.9, Pap.Oxy. 1644.12 i B.C., Herondas 2, 34.38, Philo *Spec. Leg.* (3).14, Joseph., *Ant.* XII 11 2, Plut., I 797 B – *Agis & Cleom.* IX Τῆς τε μητρὸς Ἀγησιστράτης καὶ μάμμης Ἀρχιδαμίας, I 804 A (=Ag/B VI a.xix) παρῆσαν ἥ τε μήτηρ τοῦ Ἀγίδος καὶ ἡ μάμμη, Artemid. 24.22 πατὴρ καὶ πάππος... μήτηρ καὶ μάμμη, Appian, Mith. 23, Epict. I.xvi. 28.
- ματαιολόγος iii. Telestes, Lyr. I.9 (Anth. Lyr. ed. E.Diehl) iv.B.C. Polemon, *Physiogn.* I.10 (Scriptores Physiogn. veteres, ed.C.G.F. Francius, Altenburg, 1780 p.247.5). Vett.Val. 301[1] (–ία Polycarp, Phil. ii.1, Plut., I 6 F, Vett.Val. 150[4] 257[23] 360[4], Porphyry, *abst.* 4.16, Diogenianus Epicureus 2, 16 ii A.D. in Euseb. *praep. ev.* 6.8.11. –έω Strabo II.1.19, Diogenianus II 61 in Corpus Paroem. Gr. ed. Lentsch & Schneidewin, Göttingen, 1889 p. 205.5).

- [μεμβράνα] ii. Charax 4 ii/iii A.D. (Fragm.Hist.Gr., C.Müller, Paris,1841-70, III. p.636. iv.p.669). Pap.Oxy.2156.9 c.A.D. 400. cf.Horace, Serm.ii.3.19 "sic raro scribis, ut toto non quater anno/ membranam poscas", and Gaius, Inst. ii.77 'quod in chartulis sive membranis meis aliquis scripserit, meum est'.

- μητρολῴας i. (So ℵ and most modern editors, 1Tim.i.9) In this spelling the word appears to be unique. For the T.R. μητραλοίας see Aeschyl.Eum.153, 210, Pla., Phaedo 114A πατραλοίας καὶ μητραλοίας. Lysias 10.8, Lucian, Deor.Concil.12, Phrynicus, Praep.Soph. (ed. Joannes de Borries, Lips.1911) p.25 ἔνθεν καὶ πατραλοίας καὶ μητραλοίας, ὃ τὸν πατέρα καὶ τὴν μητέρα ἀλοῶν, ὅ ἐστιν τύπτων καὶ ἐπιτρίβων. A.D. 165-170

- νεόφυτος i. = 'new convert', 'a convert newly baptized' (N.E.B.). 1Tim.iii.6. In this metaphorical sense unique. = 'newly planted vine or tree.' LXX Job.xiv.9 Ps.cxxvii (cxxviii) 3, cxliii (cxliv) 12 ὧν οἱ υἱοὶ ὡς νεόφυτα ἡδρυμμένα ἐν τῇ νεότητι αὐτῶν, Is.v.7. Pap.Cair.Zen.236.4. iii.B.C. Philo, de Virt.5.28 (ἀμπέλῳ) 21.156 (τὰ νεόφυτα τῶν δένδρων).

- νηφάλιος v., Aeschyl.Eum.107 (μειλίγματα wineless), Apollonius Rhod.4.712 (εὐχωλαί) iii B.C., Philo.Leg.ii.29, Mos.I (34)187, Sobr.2 ὅσων δημιουργὸς κακῶν ἡ μέθη, τοσούτων ἔμπαλιν ἀγαθῶν τὸ νηφάλιον, Plut., II 464C, 504.A etc, Appian, Mac.II.2.

- νομικός adj. iii. Pla. Aristot., Philostr.Vit.Soph.I.22.1 (ἀγῶνες) ed.K.L.Kayser 1871 iii A.D. Dio Chrys. II(XII)44, Hermogenes 12 (Rhetores Gr, ed. Hugo Rabe, Lips. 1913, Vol.VII p.37.19) §13, p.39.21 (στάσεις), p.44.20 (ζήτημα), M.Antonin.Imp. IV 4.2.

νομίμως iv. LXX 4 Macc.Vi.18, Pla., Thuc.,etc, Joseph., c.Apion II 13, Plut.,II 405c, Epict.III 108 (εἰ νομίμως ἤθλησας), Dio Chrys. 14 (xxxi)58,12(xlii)19, 3(iii)39, Galen, ad Hippocr. Aphor. 18 (οἱ γυμνασταὶ καὶ οἱ γε νομίμως ἀθλοῦντες), 6.488, 17(i).26.

- ξενοδοχέω i. Maximus Tyr. 26.9 a (ed.H.Hobein, Lips:1910) ii. A.D., Ps-Lucian, Amor. (47) 450. Moeris, Lexic.Att.p.248, Phrynicus (ed.C.A.Lobeck,1820) p.307 L, Cod.Just.I.3.45-1b, Late Hellenistic form of the classical 'Attic' ξενοδοκέω, cf. Hdt.6.127, Eur.Alc.582.

- οἰκοδεσποτέω i. Late Hellenistic word ((a)='predominate', Astrolog. of planets, Plut., II 908c τῶν οἰκοδεσποτούντων ἀστέρων, Ps-Lucian, Astr. 20 ὁκόσοι...ἀνθρώποισιν ἐν τῇ γενεῇ ταύτῃ οἰκοδεσποτέουσιν, Phryn. (Lobeck) p.373, Vett.Val 64.25, 67, 789 etc, Ptol.Math.Tetr. 39 (ed.J.Camerarius, Nürnberg 1535, reprint Basel 1553), Pap.Oxy.235.16 i A.D.] (b) = 'rule the household', 'be mistress of the house'. 1Tim.v.4 cf. Plut., II 271E 'Ὅπου οὖ' κύριος καὶ οἰκοδεσπότης, καὶ ἐγὼ κυρία καὶ οἰκοδέσποινα, II 613A.

- οἰκουργός iii. So ℵ*CD*G Holtzmann, Lock, Spicq, Moulton and Milligan, and most modern editors, in Tit.II.5. The only known parallel is Soranus, Gyn. I 27 (ed. V.Rose, Lips. 1882, p.18.2). οἰκουρός TR, von Soden, Eur.Hec.1277, Philo, rer.div.her.186, Plut.,II 443B, etc., Artemid. I 64, II 32 γυναῖκα εὔμορφον..., καὶ πιστὴν καὶ οἰκουρὸν καὶ πειθομένην τῷ ἀνδρί, II 35 σεμνὴν καὶ οἰκουρόν, II 54 πιστὴν καὶ οἰκουρόν (ed. Hercherus, Lips.1864).

ὀρθοτομέω ii. ὁ τὸν λόγον='handle aright,' 'rightly teach', or 'drive a straight furrow in your proclamation of the truth' (N.E.B.), 2 Tim.ii.15. Unique in this metaphorical sense. Elsewhere only in the LXX Prov.iii.6,xi.5 ἵνα ὀρθοτομῇ τὰς ὁδούς σου, δικαιοσύνη ἀμώμους ὀρθοτομεῖ ὁδούς, 'he shall direct thy paths, righteousness shall direct, or make straight or plain his paths, or ways.

- πάροινος v. Pratinas, Lyr. 1.8 (Poetae Lyr. Gr. ed.T.Bergk.Lips.1914-5) vi/v B.C. Lysias, Menander, Plut., 716 F, Lucian, Timon 55.

- πατρολῴας i. So ℵ and most modern editors, 1Tim.i.9. In this best attested spelling the word is unique. For the πατραλοίας of T.R. there are parallels both in the classics and in first and second century writers, - Aristophanes, Nub.911, Ra.274, Lysias 10.8, Plato, Joseph. Ant. XVI 111 (πατραλοίας), Lucian mort.Peregr. (21) 345, M.Antonin.Imp. VI 34.

- περιπείρω i. (='pierce' literally. Diod.Sic.16.80 ξίφεσι καὶ λόγχαις, 19.84. χάρακι i B.C., Joseph.B.J.III.7.31.τοῖς ἰδίοις ξίφεσιν, Plut.,1842 E δόρατι, Lucian, Gall.(2.)705 τοῖς ὀβελοῖς). = 'pierce' metaphorically I Tim.vi.10, ὀδύναις, Philo.Flacc.1 ἀνηκέστοις κακοῖς, Vett.Val.250".

  περιφρονέω iii. LXX 4 Macc.vi.9, vii.16, xiv.1, Thuc.,Joseph.Ant.IV.5e, Plut.,1884 D, 950 B, 169 A, II 762 E, 988 F, 1091 B, Lucian, Demosth.Enc.8.)497.

- πλέγμα i. Eur.,Pla.,Xen, Aquila and Theod. Is.xxviii.5, Philo,Somn.I (35.) 204, Joseph. Ant.II 94f.

  ποτισμός i. LXX Wi.xii.19,xiv.2. Chrysipp.Stoic.3.172 (ed.H.von Arnim, Lips.1903) 231-203 B.C. Polyb.III 112 2, Ep.Arist.III, Philo,Abr. (19.)91, Opif.Mund.128, Joseph.,B.J.II 21 3, Plut., 161 E, 349 B etc, II 92 B, 136 c, Epict.III 22 7o,Vett.Val.227?

- πρόκειμα i. IG 5 (1). 21 ii 7 (Sparta ii A.D.), Pap.Flor.68.13.16 f. A.D.172, Mitteis Chrest. 88 ii 30 (ii A.D.).

- σκέπασμα i. Plato, Aristot,Pol.7.17, Het 7(8)13.Philo de mign.Abr. (38.)215,de sacr.Abel. (25.)34,de pot.insid.(7.)19, Leg. Alleg.(85.)239, Joseph.B.J.II 83, Dio Chrys.18(xix),a, 66(xvi) 8, Plut., 1510 A.

- στόμαχος i Homer, Test. Naphth. 2.8,Philo Opif. Mund.(40.)18, Spec.Leg.(7.) 217, Dioscor. mat.med.I.17.2,42.1 etc (ed. Max Wellmann,Berlin 1906-14) I A.D., Plut., 1724 E, II 735 c etc, Epict.II 20 38, Artemid.V 89, Soranus Gyn.II.12.37, Lucian Cron.(17.) 399, Epist. 50.3, M.Ant.X 31c, 35 3, Athenaeus Mech.3 p.39 E (C.Wescher, Poliorcétique des Grecs, Paris, 1867), Galen D.U.P.I 232 19, II 314 24 (G.Helmreich, Lips.1907-9) etc.

- στρατολογέω ii. Diod.Sic.12.67.5,14.54.6 i B.C., Dion.Hal.11.24 i B.C.,Joseph. Ant. V 128, B.J.II 94 (bis), Plut., 1724 E, 410 A, 772 c, II 203 B, Artemid.II xxxi, Appian B.C. II.3, ii.31, v.7, Mithr. 87.

- συγκακοπαθέω ii. 2 Tim.i.8 Unique - except scholion on Eurip.Hec.203. (συμπαθέω Aristot, Epicur. sent.Vat.66, Justin II.xxxviii.2, Plut.,1805 B, κακοπαθέω Xen, Philo,Joseph. Ant.X 111, Dio Chrys, II (xii) 12, Zenob.V 27, 2 Cl.xix.3)

- σωφρονισμός ii. Strabo I 2a, Philo Leg. Alleg.,III. 192, Joseph. Ant.XVII 2 10, B.J. II 13, Plut., 1 338 F, 768 c, II 653 c, 712c, 961 D, Appian Pun. 65.

- τεκνογονία i. Hippocr., Aristot, Galen 15.49 (-έω Ep.ad Diogn.5.6)

- τεκνοτροφέω i. Aristot., Epicur. Fragm.525 cf. Epict.I 23 3,Plut, de amore prolis I,IV, IG XII 5.655.8 (Syros ii/iii A.D.).

  ὑδροποτέω i. LXX Dan.i.12. Hdt.,Xen., Pla.,Diosc. Mat. Med.V 71, Soranus Gyn.I 117f. (V.Rose, Lips.1882),Aelian Var.Hist.II.38 μὴ ὁμιλεῖν οἴνῳ ἀλλὰ ὑδροποτεῖν, Epict.III 13 21, Lucian bis accus.(16.)811, Macrob.(5.) 211, Moeris Lex Attic.p.346, Ammonius Gramm. Diff. p.111.v ὑδροποτέω (L.C.Valckenaer' Lips.1822) i/ii A.D.

- ὑποτύπωσις iv. Philod. Mus.p.77 (J.Kemke, Lips.1884) i B.C., Strabo II.V.18.34, Philo Abr. (15.) 71, Sextus Empiricus Pyrrh.2.79 (H.Mutschmann u.a.1912 -55) ii A.D. Hermogenes Progymn.6.20 (Rhetores Gr. ed. H.Rabe,Lips.1913 Vol.VI) ii A.D., Pollux 7.128 (ed. E.Bethe, Lips.1900 Bks.I-V, Complete in Dindorf, Lips.1824.

- ὑψηλοφρονέω i. Pollux 9.145, Schol. on Pind., Pyth.2,91 and on Eur.Hippol. 728. On this word in Photius and Suidas see W.Bauer's Wörterbuch s.v. (Also in the T.R. Rom.xi.20 where, however, NP46 etc read μὴ ὑφηλὰ φρονεῖ, and so modern editors).

- [φαιλόνης] ii. So T.R., A.Souter and W.Bauer s.v. So F. Fay.347 ii A.D. Spelt φελόνης in א 2 Tim.iv.13 and most modern editions. Spelt φαινόλης Epict.IV 8 34, Artemid.II 3, Athen.3 p.97 E, Pollux 7.61. In any case = paenula. In this genuine note Paul wants his heavy warm cloak before winter comes.

  φιλάγαθος iii. LXX Wisd. vii.11, Aristot,Polyb.VI 53 9, Ep.Arist. Philo Mos.II 9, Plut.I 37 E, II 140 c, Dio Chrys. 34 (LI) 3, Vett.Val.104?, Inscr. Wilcken,Chrest. 20 II 11 ii A.D., Pap. Oxy. 33, ii A.D.

- φίλανδρος iii. I = (a country) 'loving its men'. Aeschyl.Th.902. II=loving mascu-line habits. Soph. Fragm.1111 (Atalanta). III = 'lewd' Plato Symp.191 E. IV = 'loving one's husband' Tit.ii.4 φίλανδρους εἶναι φιλοτέκνους. Philaris Ep.132 φίλαν-δρος καὶ σώφρων (R.Hercher, Epistolographi, p.439) vi B.C., Philo de exsecr.(4.)139, Plut.,II 57 B μονολεχεῖς καὶ φίλανδροι, II 769 c φιλότεκνοι καὶ φίλανδροι, Lucian Halc. 8, Dial.Mar. 7.3 πιστή καὶ φίλανδρος Polyaenus Strat. VIII 32 34. Inscr.cit. Deissmann, L.v.O.p.267f. (Tomb of Otakilia Pola, Pergamum, time of Hadrian) ΓΥΝΑΙΚΙ ΦΙΛΑΝΔΡΩ ΚΑΙ ΦΙΛΟΤΕΚΝΩ.

133

φλύαρος ί. LXX 4 Macc.V.10, = 'nonsense', Menander 514.1.2 (Ch.Jensen, 1929) iv 32. Dion Hal. Comp. 26, Joseph. Vit. 31, Draco Strat. de metr. poet. (ed. G. Hermannus, Lips. 1812, p. 95. 26), Aristoph. Nub. 365, Epicf. II 19 10, Plut. I 861 b, 210 E, II 39 A, 701 A, Lucian Asin. (10.) 577, Diogenian II 86 (Corpus Paroem. Graec., pp. 177-250).

- φρεναπάτης iii. Herodian Gr. II 848.27 (ed. A. Lentz, 1867-70) ii A.D., Lyr. Alex. Adesp. 1.18 (Poetae Lyr. Gr. 4 ed. T. Bergk, Lips. 1882: reprint 1914-15. iii. p. 689), Pap. Grent. I.1.10 ii B.C., Pap. Lond. 5. 1677 vi A.D.

- ψευδώνυμος ί. Aeschyl. Pr. 717, Th. 670, Plut., II 479 E, 821 F, Aelian NA IX 18 (R. Hercherus, Lips. 1864) ii A.D., Epigr. Gr. 42.4, Inscr. Gr. 3. 1308. Philo, Mos. II 171 of heathen gods.

134

APPENDIX II E (supplementing II A-D in P.P.E.)

PHILO AND THE PASTORALS

1 Tim.i.15, iv.9 ἀποδοχῆς ἄξιος. fug. et invent.129 ἄξιος ἀποδοχῆς.

1 Tim.i.20, 2 Tim.i.15 ὧν ἐστιν. leg. alleg. II 105, Abel et Cain.96 ὧν ἐστιν.

ii.8 προσεύχεσθαι... ἐπαίροντας ὁσίους χεῖρας. de virtut. 57 καθαρὰς καὶ... παρθένους χεῖρας ἀνατείνας... φησιν, ἐπισκέψασθω κύριος ὁ θεὸς... " Vit. contempl. 89 χεῖρας ἀνατείνωντες... ἐπεύχονται.

ii.9 μετὰ αἰδοῦς καὶ σωφροσύνης κοσμεῖν ἑαυτάς. mutat. nom. 217 αἰδοῖ καὶ σωφροσύνη κοσμεῖται. congr. erud. 124 αἰδοῦς καὶ σωφροσύνης εὐπρεπέστατον κάλλος. spec. leg. IV 51 κοσμιότητος καὶ αἰδοῦς καὶ σωφροσύνης.

ii.10 ἐπαγγελλομένας θεοσέβειαν. Vit. contempl. 3 ἄξιον τῶν ἐπαγγελλομένων εὐσέβειαν. opif. mundi 154 θεοσέβειαν. de virtut. 54 ἡ μὲν (ἱερωσύνη) ἐπαγγέλλεται θεοῦ θεραπείαν.

iii.5 εἰ δέ τις τοῦ ἰδίου οἴκου προστῆναι οὐκ οἶδεν, πῶς ἐκκλησίας θεοῦ ἐπιμελήσεται; Somn. I 149 σπούδαζε οὖν, ὦ ψυχή, θεοῦ οἶκος γενέσθαι... ἴσως γάρ,...καὶ σὺ οἰκοδεσπότην σχήσεις· ἐπιμελούμενον τῆς ἰδίας οἰκίας.

iii.15 πῶς δεῖ ἐν οἴκῳ θεοῦ ἀναστρέφεσθαι. Somn. I 149.

iv.14 μετὰ ἐπιθέσεως τῶν χειρῶν. 2 Tim.i.6 διὰ τῆς ἐπιθέσεως τῶν χειρῶν μου. Leg. alleg. III 90 περὶ τὴν τῶν χειρῶν ἐπίθεσιν.

v.17 διπλῆς τιμῆς ἀξιούσθωσαν. Legat. ad Gai. 141 τῆς ὁμοίας τιμῆς ἠξιώσατε;

vi.3 ὑγιαίνουσιν λόγοις. 2 Tim.i.13 ὑγιαινόντων λόγων. de Abr. 223 ὑγιαίνοντας λόγους.

vi.11 δικαιοσύνην, εὐσέβειαν. Hypoth.8 δικαιοσύνης καὶ εὐσεβείας.

vi.17 εἰς ἀπόλαυσιν. de exsecr.135 εἰς ἀπόλαυσιν.

vi.20 τὴν παραθήκην φύλαξον. 2 Tim.i.12 τὴν παραθήκην μου φυλάξαι. 2 Tim.i.14 τὴν καλὴν παραθήκην φύλαξον. sacrif. Abel et Cain.60 θείων παρακαταθήκην ὀργίων οὐ παντός ἐστι· φυλάξαι. de ebriet. 213 παρακαταθήκην βιωφελεστάτων δογμάτων φυλάξαι.

2 Tim.II.9, Tit.ii.5 ὁ λόγος τοῦ θεοῦ. leg. alleg. III 170 ὁ θεοῦ λόγος.

iii.2-4 ἔσονται...φίλαυτοι, ἀλαζόνες...ἀπειθεῖς...ἀνόσιοι,...ἄσπονδοι, διάβολοι,...φιλήδονοι μᾶλλον ἢ φιλόθεοι. fug. et invent. 81 φίλαυτοι δὴ μᾶλλον ἢ φιλόθεοι. sacrif. Abel. et Cain. 3 τὸ φιλόθεον δόγμα τὸν Ἄβελ,...τὸ φίλαυτον ὁ Κάιν... sacr. Abel. et Cain. 32 ὅτι γενόμενος φιλήδονος πάντ' ἔσται ταῦτα.....ἄσπονδος... ἀλαζών.. ..διάβολος...ἀπειθής... φίλαυτος.

2 Tim. iii.7 εἰς ἐπίγνωσιν ἀληθείας ἐλθεῖν. in Flacc. 75 εἰς ἐπίγνωσιν σωτηρίας ἐλθεῖν.

    iii.8 ὃν τρόπον. Vit. Mos. 39 ὃν τρόπον.

    iii.15 ἀπὸ βρέφους. spec. leg. II 33 ἀπὸ βρέφους.

    · ibid. ἱερὰ γράμματα οἶδας. Vit. contempl. 75 ἐν τοῖς ἱεροῖς γράμμασιν. ad Gai. 195 οὐδὲ ἐνήσκηθης ταῖς ἱεροῖς γράμμασιν.

    iii.16 πρὸς ἐπανόρθωσιν. spec. leg. II 12, 107, III 76 πρὸς ἐπανόρθωσιν.

Tit. i.2 ὁ ἀψευδὴς Θεός. de ebriet. 139 ὁ ἀψευδὴς θεός.

    i.5 τούτου χάριν. leg. alleg. I 59, III 27 τούτου χάριν

    ii.4f. τὰς νέας φιλάνδρους εἶναι, φιλοτέκνους, σώφρονας, οἰκουργούς (v.l. οἰκουρούς) de execrat. 139 γυναῖκας— σώφρονας, (καὶ) οἰκουρούς καὶ φιλάνδρους. Abr. 179 φιλοτέκνων.

    ii.8 λόγον ὑγιῆ. de somn. I 79 τὸν ὑγιῆ λόγον.

    iii.4 ἡ χρηστότης καὶ ἡ φιλανθρωπία ...τοῦ Σωτῆος..Θεοῦ. Abr. 203 χρηστὸς ὢν καὶ φιλάνθρωπος ὁ θεός. leg. ad Gai. 73 χρηστότητα καὶ φιλανθρωπίαν. Abr. 176 ὁ σωτὴρ θεός. Sacrif. Abel. et Cain. 70 τῷ σωτῆρι θεῷ. vit. contempl. 87 τὸν σωτῆρα θεόν.

———

Philonis Alexandrini Opera quae supersunt recogn. Leopoldus Cohn. Editio minor, 6 Vols. Berlin 1886–1915.

NON-CHRISTIAN SECOND-CENTURY WRITERS AND THE PASTORALS

1 Tim. ii. 2 ἵνα ἥρεμον καὶ ἡσύχιον βίον διάγωμεν. Zenobius (under Hadrian) Cent. II 65 Βοιωτοὶ πρότερον βίον ἄλυπον καὶ ἥρεμον ἔχοντες. Orientis Graeci Inscriptiones selectae, ed. W. Dittenberger, 519, 10 (iii A.D.) ἥρεμον καὶ γαληνὸν τὸν βίον διαγόντων. Epict. IV. iv. 32 ἐγὼ ἤθελον ἐφ᾽ ἡσυχίας διάγειν. Lucian, Saturn. 7 τοῦτον ἥδιστον βίον διάγω. Id. Trago. 207 ἡρέμῳ ποδί.

ii. 9 ἐν...ἱματισμῷ πολυτελεῖ. Plut. Apoph. Lac. Arekidamid. vii (ed. Tauchnitz) ἱματισμὸν πολυτελῆ. (ed. Teubner has ἱμάτια πολυτελῇ here). Id. Vit. Alex. xxxix χιλίων ταλάντων ἱματισμόν.

ii. 12 διδάσκειν γυναικὶ οὐκ ἐπιτρέπω, οὐδὲ αὐθεντεῖν ἀνδρός. Proclus, Chrestom. B (Scriptores Metr. Gr., ed. Westphal, Lips. 1866) p. 249, 8 f. Θηβαῖα οὐκ ἐπιτρέπουσι γυναιξὶ μόναις τὴν περὶ αὑτῶν δίκην· κοινῆς κρίσεως ἀνδρῶν καὶ γυναικῶν γεγενημένης. Mich. Glykas (ed. I. Bekker, 1836) 270, 10 αἱ γυναῖκες αὐθεντοῦσι τῶν ἀνδρῶν. Dio Chrys. 44 (LXI) 10 ἐγυναικοκρατοῦντο οἱ Ἀτρεῖδαι. Plut. conj. praec. xxxiii. κρατεῖν δεῖ τὸν ἄνδρα τῆς γυναικός, κτλ.

ii. 12 εἶναι ἐν ἡσυχίᾳ. Dio Chrys. 49 (LXVI) 29 ἐν ἡσυχίᾳ τινὰ ὄντα. Plut., phil. esse cum princ. II τἀγαθὸν ἐν ἡσυχίᾳ τιθέμενος. Artem. Dald. Oniroerit. I. xxvi μάλιστα δ᾽ ἂν οὕτως ἐν ἡσυχίᾳ γένοιντο.

iii. 1 εἴ τις ἐπισκοπῆς ὀρέγεται, καλοῦ ἔργου ἐπιθυμεῖ. Polemo, Sophist. Declam. 35 ἔρωτι δόξης καὶ μεγάλων ἔργων ὀρεγόμενοι. Plut. vit. Artox. viii σὺ κελεύεις με τὸν βασιλείας ὀρεγόμενον ἀνάξιον εἶναι βασιλείας; Epict. Ench. 2. 2 ὅσων ὀρέγεσθαι καλόν.

iii. 13 οἱ καλῶς διακονήσαντες βαθμὸν ἑαυτοῖς καλὸν περιποιοῦνται. 2 Tim. ii. 3 καλὸς στρατιώτης. Hadrian, Sententiae (Estienne, Thes. Graec. Ling. XII. 2. 490 f. Ἐὰν καλὸς στρατιώτης γένῃ, τρίτῳ βαθμῷ δυνήσῃ εἰς πραιτώριον μεταβῆναι.

iv.9 , i.15 πάσης ἀποδοχῆς ἄξιος. Artemid.Dald.Ⅲ.xlii
πλείονος ἀποδοχῆς ἀξιωθήσονται.
iv.15 ταῦτα μελέτα, ἐν τούτοις ἴσθι. Epict.Ⅰ,i.25
ταῦτα ἔδει μελετᾶν... ἐν τούτοις γυμνάζεσθαι.
id.Ⅱ.i.29 διὰ τοῦτο λέγω πολλάκις· ταῦτα μελετᾶτε.
v.17 Οἱ καλῶς προεστῶτες πρεσβύτεροι διπλῆς
τιμῆς ἀξιούσθωσαν. Aelius Aristid. (ed.Dindorf)
Ⅰ p.134. Ἐδόκουν γὰρ οὕτως Ἀλέξανδρον...διπλῇ
τιμῇ τιμῆσαι. Dio Chrys. 27 (xliv)3 τιμάς..ὅπως
ἐκεῖνον ἐτιμήσατε. ὡς ἄνδρα ἀγαθὸν καὶ ὅσον ἔζη χρό-
νον δικαίως προεστῶτα. ῆσδε τῆς πόλεως...
v.21 χωρὶς προκρίματος. Three times in papyrus
P.Flor.Ⅰ.68, dated A.D.172.

1Tim.v.23 Μηκέτι ὑδροπότει, ἀλλὰ οἴνῳ ὀλίγῳ χρῶ δια
τὸν στόμαχον καὶ τὰς πυκνάς σου ἀσθενείας. Diosc.
D.M.M.Ⅴ.7 ὁ δὲ καλούμενος μελίτης οἶνος δίδοται
μὲν ... τοῖς ἀσθενῆ τὸν στόμαχον ἔχουσι... καὶ τοῖς
ἀσθενῆ τὴν κεφαλὴν ἔχουσι· χρήσιμος δὲ καὶ γυναι-
ξιν ὑδροποτούσαις. Aelian, Var.Hist.ii.38 γυναῖκας
μὴ ὁμιλεῖν οἴνῳ, ἀλλὰ ὑδροποτεῖν.
vi.1 τοὺς ἰδίους δεσπότας. Zenoφ.Cant.Ⅱ.81 ἐπὶ τῶν...
τοὺς ἰδίους δεσπότας, ὡς ἐπιμελουμένους, ἀφορῶν τοκ.
ibid. πάσης τιμῆς ἀξίους. Dio Chrys. 14. (xxxi)93 ἀνδρὶ
...τιμῆς ἀξίῳ. Lucian, Tox.3 θαυμαστὰ καὶ θείας τινὸς
τιμῆς ἄξια.
vi.8 ἔχοντες ..διατροφὰς .. τούτοις ἀρκεσθησόμεθα.
Epict. Ench.12.1 ἐὰν ἀμελήσω τῶν ἐμῶν, οὐχ ἕξω
διατροφάς. Dio Chrys.80 (xxx)33 τινὰς δὲ αὐτῶν μὴ
ἀρκεῖσθαι τοῖς παροῦσιν.
vi.11 ταῦτα φεῦγε· δίωκε δὲ δικαιοσύνην. 2Tim.ii22
...ἐπιθυμίας φεῦγε, δίωκε δὲ δικαιοσύνην.
Epict.Ⅳ.v.30 φύσις δ' αὕτη παντὸς τὸ διώκειν τὸ
ἀγαθόν, φεύγειν τὸ κακόν.

2Tim.ii.5 Ἐὰν δὲ καὶ ἀθλῇ τις, οὐ στεφανοῦται ἐὰν μὴ
νομίμως ἀθλήσῃ. Epict.Ⅲ.x.8 ὅ θεός σοι λέγει
'δός μοι ἐπόδειξιν, εἰ νομίμως ἤθλησας.' Galen,
ad Hippocr.Aphor.18 οἱ γυμνασταὶ καὶ οἵ γε νομίμως
ἀθλοῦντες. (cf. 4 Macc.xvii.15, ἱ A.D. θεοσέβεια...
τοὺς ἑαυτῆς ἀθλητὰς στεφανοῦσα).

138

ii.6 τὸν κοπιῶντα γεωργὸν δεῖ πρῶτον τῶν καρπῶν μεταλαμβάνειν. Zenob. Cent. V.71 εἰς δὲ τῶν οἰκέτων ἔφη μὴ μεταλήψεσθαι τὸν δεσπότην τοῦ καρποῦ.

ii.16 ἐπὶ πλεῖον προκόψουσιν. iii.9 οὐ προκόψουσιν ἐπὶ πλεῖον. Marcus Antonn. Imp., in semet ipsum I 17.8 τὸ μὴ ἐπὶ πλέον με προκόψαι.

iii. 13 προκόψουσιν ἐπὶ τὸ χεῖρον. Zenob. Cent. III.82 κατὰ τῶν ἐπὶ τὸ χεῖρον προκοπτόντων ἀεί. Joseph. B.J. VI.1.1 τὰ ... τῶν Ἱεροσολύμων πάθη προύκοπτε καθ' ἡμέραν ἐπὶ τὸ χεῖρον. Id. Ant. XX.9.4 Προκοπτόντων πάντων ἐπὶ τὸ χεῖρον.

iv.3 κνηθόμενοι τὴν ἀκοήν. Plut., de superstit. v οὐ τρυφῆς ἕνεκα καὶ κνήσεως ὤτων. Lucian, bis acc.1 οὐδ' ὅσον κνήσασθαι τὸ οὖς, φασί, σχολὴν ἄγων. Id. de salt. 2. (=266) τὸ ὅμοιον πεπονθὸς τοῖς τὰ ὦτα πτερῷ κνωμένοις. cf. Moeris, Lex Attic. (ed. Koch, 1830, p. 215) κνεῖν Ἀττικῶς, κνήθειν Ἑλληνικῶς.

iii.16 (γραφὴ) ὠφέλιμος ... πρὸς ἐπανόρθωσιν, πρὸς παιδείαν. Epict. III.21.16 οὕτως ὠφέλιμα γίνεται τὰ μυστήρια ... ὅτι ἐπὶ παιδείᾳ καὶ ἐπανορθώσει τοῦ βίου κατεστάθη.

Tit. i.11 οἵτινες ὅλους οἴκους ἀνατρέπουσιν. Plut. Vit. Timol. xxii τὰς οἰκίας ... τῶν τυράννων ἀνέτρεψαν. Lucian, Hermotim. 33 (=774) ὅμοιον ... τοῖς τῶν παιδίων οἰκοδομήμασιν, ἃ κατασκευάσαντες ἐκεῖνοι ἀσθενῆ εὐθὺς ἀνατρέπουσιν. ibid. διδάσκοντες ἃ μὴ δεῖ αἰσχροῦ κέρδους χάριν. Dio Chrys. 14 (xxxi) 67 τὸ μηδὲν αἰσχρὸν αἱρεῖσθαι κέρδους ἕνεκα.

ii.4 φιλάνδρους ... φιλοτέκνους. Plut. Amat. xxii φιλότεκνοι, καὶ φίλανδροι. Marble tombstone of Otakilia Polla (Pergamum, time of Hadrian, cit. Deissmann, L.v.O. p. 267f.) ΤΗ ΓΛΥΚΥΤΑΤΗ ΓΥΝΑΙ- ΚΙ ΦΙΛΑΝΔΡΩ ΚΑΙ ΦΙΛΟΤΕΚΝΩ ΣΥΜΒΙΩΣΑΣΗ ΑΜΕΜΠΤΩΣ ΕΤΗ Λ.

ii.12 ἵνα...σωφρόνως καὶ δικαίως καὶ εὐσέβως ζῆσω-
μεν. Dio Chrys. 73 (xxiii) 7 δικαίως ζῆν καὶ φρονί-
μως καὶ σωφρόνως. Plut. adv. Colot. ii τὸ δ' εὖ
ζῆν ἐστι κοινωνικῶς ζῆν καὶ φιλικῶς καὶ σωφρόνως
καὶ δικαίως.

ii.8 λόγον ὑγιῆ. Dio Chrys. i. 49 ἱερὸν καὶ ὑγιῆ λόγον.
Marcus Antonin. Imp., in semet ips. VIII 30 ὑγιεῖ λόγῳ
χρῆσθαι.

iii.3 πλανώμενοι, δουλεύοντες ἐπιθυμίαις καὶ ἡδοναῖς. 2 Tim. iii. 4 φιλήδονοι μᾶλλον ἢ φιλόθεοι.
Dio Chrys. 4 (iv) 115 πλανῶνται...δεδουλωμένοι
δὲ ἡδοναῖς, φιλήδονοι. (cf. Porphyr. ad Mar-
cellam 14, ed. Nauck, p. 283, 20f. iiiAD. ἀδύνατον
τὸν αὐτὸν φιλόθεόν τε εἶναι καὶ φιλήδονον).

APPENDIX III

BIBLIOGRAPHY

Special editions and Introductions to the Pastorals.

(Supplementing those on p. 179 f. of P.P.E.)

E. Bosio, *Le epistole pastorali a Timoteo e a Tito*, Florence, 1911; E. F. Brown, *The Pastoral Epistles*, (Westminster Commentaries), London, 1917; A. E. Hillard, *The Pastoral Epistles of St. Paul*, London, 1919; E. Bisseker, *The Pastoral Epistles* (A Commentary on the Bible . . . A. S. Peake), London, 1920; C. H. Erdman, *The Pastoral Epistles of St. Paul*, Philadelphia, 1923; W. Lock, *The Pastoral Epistles* (International Critical Commentary), Edinburgh, 1924; H. L. Strack and Paul Billerbeck, (Kommentar zum N.T., iii, pp. 643sq.), München; T. H. Haering, *Die Pastoralbriefe*, Stuttgart, 1928; H. C. G. Moule, *The Second Epistle to Timothy*, London, 1928; P. Delatte, *Les Épîtres de Saint Paul replacées dans le milieu historique*, II, pp. 473–586, Tours, 1929; H. W. Creutzberg, *De tweede brief aan Timotheus*, La Haye, 1930; H. Meinerz, *Die Pastoralbriefe des heiligen Paulus*, (*Die heilige Schrift des N.T.*, Fr. Tillmann), Bonn, 1931; B. Vincent, *The Pastoral Epistles for To-day* . . . , London, 1932; P. Leo, *Das anvertraute Gut; eine Einführung in den ersten Timotheusbrief (Die urchristliche Botschaft*, xv), Berlin, 1935; Sailer, *Der erste Brief Pauli an Timotheus*, Augsburg, 1936; J. Behm, (*Einl. in das N.T.*, pp. 195 f.) Leipzig, 1936; M. R. James, *The Pauline and Pastoral Epistles*, (Aldine Bible) London, 1936; E. A. Gardiner, *The later Pauline Epistles*, London, 1936; E. F. Scott, *The Pastoral Epistles* (The Moffat N.T. Commentary) 1936[1]–1947[5]; R. Falconer, *The Pastoral Epistles*, Oxford, 1937; H. Molitor, *Die Pastoralbriefe* (Herder's Bibelkommentar, Die Heilige Schrift, xv), Fribourg, 1937; G. Bardy, *Épîtres Pastorales* (La Sainte Bible, xii), Paris, 1938; J. Jeremias, *Die Briefe an Timotheus und Titus*, Göttingen, 1937; M. Dibelius, *Die Pastoralbriefe* (Handbuch zum N.T. xiii), Tübingen, 1931, 1955[1] revised by H. Conzelmann; H. Rossier, *Étude sur la première tÉptre à Timothée*, Vevey, 1938; *Étude sur l' Épître à Tite*, Vevey, 1921; E. Hastings, *The Pastoral and Johannine Epistles*, (Speaker's Bible), 1943; C. Spicque, *Saint Paul, Les Épîtres Pastorales*, (Etudes Bibliques), Paris, 1947; B. S. Easton, *The Pastoral Epistles*, London, 1948; A. Boudou, *S. Paul, Les Épîtres Pastorales*, 1950; P. Dornier, *Les Épîtres de S. Paul à Timothée et à Tite*, Paris, 1951; P. de Ambroggi, *Epistola I e II a Timoteo e Tito*, 1953; E. K. Simpson, *The Pastoral Epistles*, London, 1954; Fred. D. Gealy, *Commentary on the Pastoral Epistles* (The Interpreter's Bible, Vol. xi), New York and Nashville, 1955; Donald Guthrie, *The Pastoral Epistles and the Mind of Paul*, London, 1956; Donald Guthrie, *The Pastoral Epistles, an Introduction and Commentary*, London, 1957; A. R. C. Leany, *The Epistles to Timothy, Titus and Philemon*, London, 1960.

141